MIKE TYSON TRIED TO KILL MY DADDY!

By Mitchell Rose

MIKE TYSON TRIED TO KILL MY DADDY!

This book is based on a true story.

First Edition

Cover Designed by Angela Olverson

ISBN 13: 978-0-9797797-1-8

TABLE OF CONTENTS

FOREWORD

Mitchell Rose came to my office today. There was nothing unusual about that, for over the last fifteen years we have consistently kept in touch. What was unusual was when he produced a manuscript and said "look Epstein, this is the book I was telling you about."

Of course I was immediately skeptical. I have known Mitchell Rose the criminal defendant, Mitchell Rose the struggling boxer, Mitchell Rose the hustler, Mitchell Rose the small business man, but Mitchell Rose the author?

What was even more shocking was, as Mitchell sat in my office taking numerous phone calls on his wireless, I began reading from a random spot in the manuscript and found myself immediately transfixed by his words.

Who would have thought that Mitchell could write such an interesting account? After all I met him in early 1992 when I was a young Legal Aid lawyer (i.e. Public Defender), in Brooklyn, New York when I was assigned to represent Mitchell on an armed robbery case.

I had been at the Legal Aid society for about two years, when I was just given permission by my supervisors to start defending cases involving allegations of serious felonies. Mitchell's was one of my first. I had inherited his case from a veteran defender who was only too happy to lighten his load by giving a young eager co-worker a nice "meaty" case.

And what a case it was! From the start it had all the trappings of an epic legal battle. A young man was accused of a very serious crime-armed robbery, even though there was no allegation that he handled a weapon or ever demanded money from the victim. Instead, the accusation was that he was the "look out guy". Could this young man, with such an easy smile and (apparently) no criminal record actually have been involved in a brazen daylight armed robbery right in the crowded downtown Brooklyn area? Or could this be another case of a young black man who was "at the wrong place at the wrong time" (as I had already heard, and have since heard, hundreds of times).

Being the young and eager advocate that I was (as opposed to the middle age and eager advocate I have become), I immediately sprang into action. For not was I only young and eager, there was something from the get go that attracted me to Mitch. From the first conversation you forget about his size, obvious physical strength, deep voice, and instead focus on his easy smile, intelligence and sense of humor. Right away I could sense that despite his desperate situation, Mitch had a bright future.

It appeared to me that considering his lack of criminal history, Mitch's bail was excessive. Therefore, I filed a habeas corpus petition in an attempt to have his bail reduced. The Supreme Court Judge agreed and within days Mitch was bailed out and back on the streets.

Nevertheless, Mitch's problems were far from over. Shortly thereafter he found himself indicted by a Grand Jury for First Degree robbery, a charge that, back then, carried a maximum sentence of 8 to 25 years.

Man, how I looked forward to the upcoming trial, but man was I soon disappointed to find out that

I had to get off of his case. It had come to my supervisor's attention that one of the other co-defendant's had already been assigned a Legal Aid lawyer, thus, creating a conflict of interest (since The Legal Aid society is technically one large law firm). Therefore, despite my most valiant efforts in arguing to keep Mitch's case, I had no choice, but to request that the court relieve me and assign different counsel to Mitch.

However, the story did not end for me there. Many months later Mitch was on trial on the tenth floor of the Court house on Schermerhorn Street in downtown Brooklyn. It so happened that I had many cases pending on the same floor. Mitch's jury was out for at least four days before they reached their verdict, and I would commonly see Mitch just sitting out in the hall waiting for that jury to come back with a decision. If I had a few extra minutes between cases i would just sit with him and talk.

I had explained to Mitch that the Judge presiding over his trial, Judge Sheldon Greenberg, had a very distinct reputation. It was known amongst the lawyers in Brooklyn, that Judge Greenberg would give a defendant the fairest trial he could get in the county, if not the whole city. But, if you lost, he felt perfectly justified in handing out the maximum punishment-which he invariably did on those rare instances where the defendant was convicted.

On hindsight I can only imagine what was in Mitchell's head those many days sitting alone on a bench outside of Judge Greenberg's courtroom on that 10th floor of 120 Schermerhorn. I could only imagine that every mistake and bad choice he had made was replaying in Mitch's' mind. I am certain now that he thought about all the lost opportunities he had and would especially have if he were to be convicted. I am certain that he questioned all of his beliefs and attitudes and thought if he only got this break he would make the most of it.

Who knew that it was actually a book that was inside of Mitchell's head.

By Attorney Epstein

Thank you to:

Angela Olverson, aka AngieO, graphic designer, Ms.AngieO@yahoo.com, Master Editor Noreen Mallory, Editor Diane school teacher, Editor Arlene school teacher, proof reader Jordan Salmon. Most importantly thank you to my wife Delores Rose for giving me my first editor Ms. Jackson. I want to say God bless my four children Adrian Alleyne, Rheavonni Rose, Delores Katlin Rose and my, most recently born, son Mitchell Champion Rose, Jr.

INTRODUCTION

I grew up in the streets of New York City. "Do or Die" Bed Stuy Brooklyn is where I am from. I have seen just about every hustle that is out there but when I started boxing, I saw that hustlers aren't just running the streets. Hustlers are running businesses, corporations and sports. And hustlers are running the sport of boxing.

When I beat the popular fighter Butterbean, I stunned the world of boxing when I knocked him out in Madison Square Garden in front of 18,000 people. That four round bout with Butterbean is considered one of the greatest four rounders in history. As a rising heavyweight, a lot of people showed me love after that. Newspaper and television reporters were talking about it. I was excited too and looking forward to whatever was next for me in boxing. But what I quickly found out is that boxing is a lot more than power punches and championship belts. Boxing is shady business.

"The Man Who Beat Butterbean But Now Has to Beat These City Streets" is my story of how I grew up on the streets of New York hustling, robbing and selling drugs before I turned my life around. As a teen, you will see how my brushes with the law and eventually a stint in a youth facility influenced me and helped me to grow as a person. I saw and did a lot on the streets. But when I got into boxing, some of the things that happened to me are pretty unbelievable. There are so many things, from the way bouts are organized to how much time certain opponents get to prepare for a fight to underhanded deals that make boxing shady. That is not even considering the racism. People may not want to hear it but yes, racism exists in boxing. And my fight with Butterbean is a good example.

At the time, he was considered the "Great White Hope". Many white boxing fans looked at him to become the next heavyweight champion. While the racial overtones are not always overt in boxing, they are definitely there. As white fans supported their "Great White Hope", black fans supported me. This is not new. All of the great black fighters from the past - Joe Louis, Jack Johnson etc. - all of them experienced the venom that spews when race enters the boxing ring. So my experience wasn't new. And even minus the subtleties, as a boxer, when you are in the ring, you hear what people are saying. White fans yell things like "fuck that black guy up". Black fans yell "whip that cracker ass". It's crazy but this is boxing, one of the grittiest sports around.

My boxing career is full of moments and events and the Butterbean fight was just the beginning. For one, the media's coverage of the fight was overwhelming. News of my upset was worldwide. All of the major sports networks and a bunch of local stations across the country aired stories about my victory. Sports writers and columnists were talking about it. The boxing world was buzzing. This fight was HUGE! It even landed Butterbean a guest spot on the Jay Leno show. And about a year later, Butterbean was featured on Playstation's "Knockout Kings" game. To this day, kids know him from playing that game. But at the same time that people in boxing were hyping up Butterbean, I was getting dissed. Apparently, it wasn't in the plan for me, the little known opponent, to win the fight never mind knock Butterbean out. He was supposed to be the "King of the Four Round", not me.

I became infamous in boxing after I beat Butterbean. Promoters did not want to touch me and it was hard getting a fight. I was considered a spoiler because I upset a favorite. I became a feared boxer that no manager wanted to put his fighter up against. But I continued fighting and had a loyal following. These fans are still with me now. After ultimately participating in three Golden Glove competitions and ten pro bouts, I retired in 1998 to raise my family. But not before being in another fight that would cause a media circus.

After a night of socializing, I ended up in a street fight with none other than Mike Tyson. We got into it in front of a club in Brooklyn. Mike banged me up a little bit and damaged an expensive item of mine setting off another battle between us. Once word of this incident seeped out, the press swarmed around me like bees. Kendra Farm from New York's Channel 4 News was one of the first to respond. She wanted the story and was one of the first reporters that I talked to. Before you knew it, there were newspaper articles and columns, radio and TV appearances. Eventually, I even appeared on Wendy Williams' radio show. I was so hyped up on that show it was crazy! I had filed a police report about the incident with Mike Tyson. And I also had a lawyer, Sanford Rubenstein - the same lawyer who represents Al Sharpton and at one time, Abner Louima.

With Sanford, the Tyson situation was at a whole new level. For starters, we filed a sixty six million dollar lawsuit against Mike Tyson for pain and suffering and punitive damages. This eventually brought us to Court TV and CNN. Together, Sanford and I were on those networks talking about the incident. However, from day one, officials, especially in Brooklyn's District

Attorney's office, acted as if I was a gold digger just trying to get Mike's money. The papers were reporting the story as if I went after Mike. Tyson knew the deal and so did I. But the truth was not getting out. Just like with the Butterbean fight, it seems certain people had an agenda and Mitch Rose was not the beneficiary.

I pursued Tyson seeking an apology and restitution for what I lost in the fight. So it only made sense to show up at the press conference for the upcoming Tyson / Lennox Lewis fight. Up until then, from the Butterbean fight on up to my fight outside the club with Tyson, my side of the story was not being told. My voice was not being heard. Now, it was time to shout. What occurred at that press conference is legendary and caused a press frenzy. I was told that NBC's Saturday Night Live even spoofed the press conference incident. I remember being at home and the TV was turned on to the Regis Philbin show and Regis' co-host, Kelly, was reading from a newspaper write up about the incident. Then she said "Way to go Mitch" and that just made me smile.

With "*MIKE TYSON TRIED TO KILL MY DADDY!*" I want to show how the world of boxing truly is. As one of the most unregulated sports, if not the most unregulated, boxing is in need of help. I support the Muhammad Ali Act, an act the former champion boxer proposed that would set up tighter rules for the sport. It would address the injustices in the sport such as fight preparation time, unequal pay and judging. I am not sure where this Act stands or if it even still exists. If not, it should or something like it.

I have been boxing since I was a teenager. For anybody who is thinking about getting into boxing, I hope that this book gives them insight into the dos and don'ts of the sport. You may want boxing but the question is, "Does boxing want you?" I still box today but I do not really see myself in another heavyweight championship bout. But, you never know. Butterbean is still fighting and has won a bunch of fights, however, the opponents he has had are really questionable. Many of them have been guys with little skills, barely fighters at all. The first guy I fought after Butterbean, Monte Barrett, who eventually fought for the heavyweight championship in November 2006. He was TKOed in the eleventh round. And Gerald Noble, who I fought after Monte, just recently fought for the heavyweight championship in Germany. At the height of the hoopla between me and Butterbean and then Mike Tyson, much has been said and written about me. But you have not heard from me - until now. My mama used to say, "Boy, quit talking that crazy talk." I am the man that beat Butterbean and this is my story.

CHAPTER 1: THE PJs

I remember the first day I moved into the projects called LaFayette Gardens in Brooklyn, New York. It was in 1971 and I was two years old. I'll never forget being in the kitchen, and seeing a big box with gray cotton fabrics scattered all over the floor. I remember sitting on the floor playing with the fabrics and beating up the box, which was probably the time I discovered my boxing abilities. Although, at the time, I didn't know I'd become a boxer later on in life. And to me it is amazing how I can remember so far back like that!

Back then, I didn't know how we landed in the projects. As a matter of fact, it wasn't until thirty years later that I found out the story of how we had gotten burned out of an apartment complex on Quincy Ave. How that fire got started, I never knew. I do, however, recall personally burning our apartment in LaFayette Gardens back in 1980 when I was about ten or eleven.

I was in our apartment, while my family was at my Aunt Robbie's playing cards. She lived on Gates Avenue in Brooklyn. My mother and her three sisters usually would have card games on the weekends. I was in the back bedroom smoking a cigarette looking out the window. I remember that a white sheet on the surface of the window ledge was used to seal the cracks in the window to stop the cold air from coming into the apartment.

I dropped the cigarette on the bottom of the bed and it caught fire. I thought I had successfully put it out with my hand, but later found out that a spark had still been burning inside the mattress. I left the bedroom and went over to my Aunt Robbie's house. By the time I arrived at my aunt's, my mom was screaming at me hysterically.

"Mitcha, as my mom would call me with her southern accent, Rayshawn called and said our apartment is on fire!" Rayshawn, who was the same age as I was, was our next door neighbor and our mothers were good friends.

I played dumb and said I didn't know what happened. My mother just looked at me real hard, and all of our relatives were looking at us in a daze. The fireman's report determined that the fire had started by the window. Since the bed was planted right by the window, my alibi was that the sheet on the window must have caught fire by someone throwing a cigarette out of their window and igniting the bed, because the sheet was hanging down on the floor next to the bed. Knowing that people in the projects are always throwing objects out of the windows, it was very possible that this accident could have happened this way. There were a lot of incidents where all kinds of material and debris were falling on window seals from top floors. Nevertheless, I was exaggerating and lying with this particular incident.

My mother looked at me, like she knew I was lying but the damage had been done. All the furniture was burned in all three rooms, the beds, my bike and all of our clothes. I did find all of my savings still inside the large can that I turned into my piggie bank. I had about forty dollars worth of change inside of it. My family and I had to sleep at my aunt's house for a couple of days. We also slept for a few days at our next door neighbor, Rayshawn's family's apartment. Eventually our apartment was fixed, renovated and painted.

My mother appeared to be very curious about the whole situation and she knew that I was a spoiled brat that stayed in some kind of foolishness or trouble but I was also her baby boy and she loved me to the point where she would let me get away with almost anything. She was a single parent, and didn't have much control over my three sisters and me. She was poor and stressed out most of the time worrying about where we would get our next meal.

My mom left the racially divided town of Montgomery, Alabama in 1962, and came to New York City to find work and better opportunities. Within a couple of months she had met our father at a house party, where he was playing guitar for a band called "The Disco Boys". In 1966, four years after my mother and father met, my twin sisters, Anita and Urita were born. Anita came out fine but Urita had some learning disabilities. Then a year later, my sister Keisha was born. She was a weird kid who sucked her thumb and liked to eat candy and bubble gum off of the ground. And a year after that, I was born. We were all tight, so tight that all four of us could sit on one couch together sucking our thumbs following Keisha's example. My three sisters added synchronized rocking back and forth on the couch to their daily thumb sucking sessions. Sucking their thumbs became a long term habit for Keisha and Urita. Anita eventually broke her habit and I did not stop sucking my thumb until I was about twelve years old when I started hanging out with my boys regularly. They would joke and tease me and at that time I was supposed to be "too cool" so I had to dig down deep and break the habit.

Six years prior to my sisters and I being born, my mother had a son named Ricky Joe, who she left down South with her mother and father. She left him with our grandparents so that she could go to New York City to find work. For a woman without a lot of cash, it would have been very difficult to deal with working and trying to raise a child on her own.

My mother and father split up when I was about three years old, leaving me fatherless at a very early age. Our father, Ricky Ricardo Rose, is of Jamaican descent but since he was a baby he was raised in Panama. His parents migrated to Panama to find work at the Panama Canal.

Years later, when I was about ten, my mother gave him visitation rights. I recall him bringing us to his apartment in Brownsville, Brooklyn every weekend until I was about twelve. He tried to show some fatherly love by occasionally taking me to the park to challenge me to a game of stickball. But these get togethers were very limited. He was, from what I understand, too busy trying to pursue his music career as a guitarist. Unfortunately, a lot of black fathers found ways to avoid being around their children and hiding from their responsibilities. It is a pattern that became a fad for black men that is very difficult to understand because your kid is your blood like your mother or your brother. So why would you betray your own flesh and blood? I do know he was a very poor man who worked for six dollars an hour for twenty something years as a messenger, and when he got close to being eligible for a pension plan, his job laid him off before he could qualify.

My father put in twenty years of hard work and dedication for that company and they still betrayed him. My father was a very religious man who didn't believe in breaking the law. He was the type of guy that wore three outfits for ten years repeatedly. My father was such an honest man, he told me a story one day that he was so hungry that he stole a pack of franks from the supermarket but after that he felt so guilty and embarrassed that he never stole again in his life. And I believe him because I have the same tendencies. I recall being so broke when I saw my friend Craig flashing a wad of money that I asked him to borrow $20. He sucked his teeth and said he couldn't do anything for me. I felt so embarrassed and ashamed of myself that I never asked anybody to borrow money ever again. My father didn't even try to fight back for what they did to him. He told me when I asked why didn't he challenge the corporation, instead he retired and found peace playing his guitar in the train station all over mid-town for tips. He told me he saved up $15,000 in two years. The most he ever had in his entire 71 years of life.

Growing up in the projects was very destructive to me, due to negative peer pressure. By the time I was seven years old, I was smoking and drinking. I would see the older guys drinking 40 ounces of Old English 800 and Colt 45. Seeing Billy Dee Williams in Colt 45 beer commercials didn't make things better, because he influenced damn near the whole urban community to drink malt liquor. Beer companies profits increased dramatically from such commercials. Before the recycling program came out in the eighties, Colt 45 cans littered all the ghettos in the United States. With the recycling program, you could trade in your used cans and bottles for five cents which made the streets a whole lot cleaner.

Weed smoking was also common in the projects. If you walked down the stairs, the exits were littered with joint roaches all the way down from the top floor to the bottom floor. My homeboys and I would walk up and down the stairs every other day collecting the leftover roaches then rolling them up into one big spliff. Then we would put our quarters together and buy a 40 ounce of Colt 45 or Old English 800. I guess that was the beginning of our addiction, because we eventually started playing hooky from school at least once or twice a week. Once you start using drugs and alcohol, you open up a path for other negativity.

It was 1977, the year the big blackout occurred in New York City, and my homeboys and I all lived in the same project building. At this time I was eight, and Darryl aka Rahiem was nine. His brother, Erving, who was my best friend, was seven. June was eight, and Melvin, aka Divine who was the oldest of the group, was eleven. I lived on the eighth floor, Rahiem and Erving lived on the seventh floor, and June and Melvin both lived on the fourteenth floor. June and I were friends first; we had been in the same class from the first to third grade.

June was a short, chubby guy like me, and Melvin was a muscular guy who knew how to fight very well for his age. A lot of the local kids were afraid of him because of the way he looked. He had a black tooth, which he said came from electric tape that he had put on his teeth playing around. The tape got stuck and remained there for a few years, which made him look like a scary dude. We also had a "sometimes" friend in the neighborhood named Norman, who was eight years old. He'd take us downtown into the shopping area and show us how easy it was to walk out of department stores like A&S Strauss and Gimbels with skateboards and toys.

Over time our shoplifting grew progressively

worse. We started stealing electronic games, such as Pac Man and portable sport games such as baseball and hockey. You name the toy, we had it. We had all the superhero toys like Spiderman and Batman and Robin to play with. The other kids in our neighborhood were shocked. They couldn't believe the toys we were able to have, expensive things worth $75 -$100. We were all from the average black families who couldn't afford such expensive toys, maybe one or two but ten or fifteen types of expensive toys - never. The older kids, thirteen to fifteen years old, were so jealous of us they started beating us up and taking our toys.

After about six months of shoplifting toys, we started taking clothes. We'd go into a dressing room with two pair of pants, and we'd put a pair on under our own pants. Then we'd bring out the second pair and return them to the rack. The salespeople wouldn't even notice any items missing. That became our daily recreation. It was exciting. We didn't have football or baseball teams in our community to occupy our time; so we made stealing our sport.

However, I was the one who was always leery about stealing. I would con Erving into taking most of my toys and clothes. Erving was a skinny little kid who wasn't afraid to take chances. Because people thought he wasn't playing with a full deck, years later, Erving eventually landed in King's County Hospital in the G Building which was especially designated for mentally ill people. Erving used to kill dogs and cats on a regular basis by throwing dogs off of twenty story buildings and swinging cats around in the air and then banging their heads on the ground about five or six times until they went into convulsions and died. His activity had gotten so bad that I started coaching him by telling him he had to break his record. One day he would kill five cats then I would tell him he had to kill six in order to break his cat killing record.

When we were in the store shoplifting, I would pass my stuff to Erving and say, "Hey, get this for me, Erv." And since he was so kindhearted, he'd just take the stuff from me. He was like my henchman. Although, there were times when I had to fend for myself.

As we continued our hustle boosting, we eventually ran into other young guys who were into more advanced activities, like pick pocketing. In 1980, as my crew and I were getting on the G train at the Classon Avenue Station to do our daily activity, we unexpectedly met three guys; Tarzan, Eyes and Gary. Tarzan was the oldest; he was about fourteen. They called him Tarzan because he looked like a monkey and ran really fast. He would jump over cars and fences to get away from the police. They lived in the same neighborhood as we did.

These guys were into all types of crimes, from pick pocketing to snatching pocketbooks and gold chains. They were very bold criminals, and on that day, we followed them all over the city. They introduced us to some things we would've never thought of or even imagined doing in our wildest dreams. Most of that day, they used us as guinea pigs and bait.

We would block the path of a pedestrian while they pick pocketed the victim. They would lift a lady's wallet right out of her pocketbook with such swiftness that she wouldn't even know it, and by the time she did, we would be long gone. There were different amounts of money and all types of credit cards. Since we were so young, we didn't know what to do with the credit cards; we just threw them away. Eventually my crew and I learned how to pick pocket, but I never got as good as they were because I was heavy handed and careless.

People would turn around, scream and yell at me, "Get your hand out my pocketbook, you bum! You bastard! You this, you that!" Especially the black women, they would curse a little snot nose guy like myself out. Can you imagine a little chubby guy with a dirty t-shirt with juice stains, digging into your pocket or pocketbook? People thought I was silly and a lost case.

When we were working with Tarzan, Gary and Eyes, they treated us unfairly. Sometimes, at the end of the day, we might have made four to five hundred dollars and they'd only give us twenty or thirty dollars each because they were the skillful ones that did all the pick pocketing. All of us were supposed to split the profits equally, but sometimes they wouldn't give us anything and would go home laughing at us. We, in turn, would have to go home looking puzzled and hungry.

After working with them for about three months, my crew and I started getting better, and we decided to go solo. Tarzan, Gary and Eyes started getting jealous once they saw how good we had gotten and that we were able to fend for ourselves. We started snatching our own gold chains and bracelets from pedestrians in Midtown. We used to go out specifically looking for bangles bracelets because we considered them profitable. Erving was the first one of us that had the heart to take them, then Rahiem and I followed.

In 1982, I snatched a couple of bangles from a Jamaican woman on 41st Street. Only Rahiem was with me because Erving was in jail. The bangles were worth about two hundred and fifty dollars each. Gary saw me and got really angry, because he saw how big they were, and I had gotten them before he did. I turned, looked at him and laughed in his face, which he didn't take very well.

Gary made it back to LaFayette Gardens before me and Rahiem. He went and found two of the older criminals in the neighborhood, "Punch", who was no more than seventeen, and "Bush" who was about sixteen and considered the Tooky Williams of Brooklyn. Tooky Williams was a notorious guy from California that killed four people. Governor Schwarzenegger wouldn't grant him clemency and was killed by lethal injection. They waited for us to get off the G Train.

When Gary saw us, he yelled to Punch and Bush, "There they go!" They started rushing toward us.

Since I had always been a fast thinker, I pulled out one bangle and passed it to Rahiem like a quarterback at a football game. "Go Rahiem!" I yelled to him.

Rahiem took off running, but was tackled immediately. They thought he had all the merchandise, but Gary recognized my deception.

As I ran through the back of the projects, Gary shouted, "He's got the other one!"

The back door was locked, but there was a hole in the side of the door window, and I dove through it. With Punch still on my heels, I ran up eight flights of stairs. Punch eventually made it up the steps but by then I'd already made it inside my apartment. I peered out the door through the peephole, holding the bangle in my hand, smiling and laughing.

Sounding like a kid teasing another kid with a

piece of candy, I said, "You can't get me, you can't get me, you broke motherfucker!" Then I slammed the door behind me.

The next day, I took the bangle to the pawnshop and got $250.00 for it. When I saw Rahiem, I told him it was too bad he had allowed them to take his bangle, and with LaFayette Gardens' Day being the next day, I had to get fresh. I bought a beige jail suit, a matching outfit that was similar to what inmates wore in jail, and some British walkers. Back in the early 80s, that was one of the fads and styles in the hood. The majority of teenagers wore them to be fashionable and look cool and LaFayette Gardens' Day was the place to show off. It was like a holiday celebration for the people in the projects.

Then I went to the back of the projects where they threw the parties, fronting with my new outfit on trying to impress the girls and the guys that I am a successful crook. The parties were always crowded with about a 100 or maybe 200 people and mostly kids and teenagers attended. Everyone was dancing, laughing, drinking beer and liquor, smoking weed and having a good time. You had different DJs that wanted to make it big one day like DJ Mr. Cee. He's the only DJ from around the way that made it to the mainstream industry. He currently plays for Hot 97 FM in New York. It was also rappers who did their thing on the mic. At the parties, they had battles against each other and became neighborhood heroes. And back in 1982 when rap just really started becoming popular, I was too shy and cool to dance, so I just played the wall drinking a 40 oz of Old Gold watching brothers do the electric boogie and freak style and the girls do the bump and the smurf. Everybody was having a good time all night until 12am, 1am or 2am in the morning or until the cops came. The cops made the DJs pack up. It was that or somebody either got shot or stabbed. This particular night was Lafayette Garden's Day and the two neighborhood bullies, Punch and Bush arrived and everyone started getting afraid and nervous. Punch and Bush, the evil villains, had to always make a statement and ruin everybody's night and bust a shot up in the air and made everybody scatter for dear life. People were screaming, running and knocking each other over, they created a big stampede. When the park was cleared, some people were sprawled out on the ground banged and bruised up like the herds of animals running in the movie the "Lion King".

* * *

Slowly but surely everyone I knew started going to jail or upstate to juvenile facilities. I was the last to go. At the age of 12, when I went to see the judge, I was ordered to go into a group home by the court. By the time I went, I already had about three or four arrests on my record. I caught another case with some of my boys.

In 1982, my boys and I raided a pharmacy by snatching a whole bunch of cigars called Tiparillos. That day, I was the only one that got caught. This chubby Black security guard chased us about ten blocks but I ran out of air near the train station in downtown Brooklyn on Holt Street.

Me with Dad,Ricky Ricardo Rose, and 3 sisters Anita, Urita and Keisha

My father Ricky playing the guitar in train station

CHAPTER TWO: SPOFFORD

The group home was in the Bronx near Yankee Stadium. My first night there, I jumped out the window and escaped. At this time, my family, who knew I was a bad kid making some bad choices, shook their heads at my return. They didn't have any control over me. While at home, I fell right back into the same aspects of life that I knew - robbing, stealing, drinking and smoking.

A couple months later, two detectives came to our apartment and got me. They took me to Spofford, a juvenile facility in the Bronx. Spofford is a holding place for offenders until their counselor or probation officer finds an opening in a placement facility. My mother was down south in Alabama at the time, so my Aunt Ann appeared in court on her behalf. They sentenced me to twelve months at a camp called Great Valley in upstate New York. My Aunt Ann broke down crying in court.

Prior to going to Spofford, I was held inside the court house in the back room. They took me in the back of the court and fed me a cold bologna sandwich before shipping me off to Spofford. I stayed there for only three months. Life still felt like one big joke to me. It seemed like going to jail or a juvenile facility like all my homies was the ultimate cool thing to do. It was almost like if you didn't go to jail like everybody else in the hood, you were nobody. You were not a part of a special culture. You were like an outcast, and that is tradition in the ghetto.

Spofford was a pretty fascinating experience for me. I anticipated the challenge and became an extremely macho guy. It was cool to see guys walking into the cafeteria with an orange jumpsuit on, bouncing the food up and down on their trays as they walked by. I have to admit the greasy eggs that we were served three times a week were really tasty.

There was this one guy named Bruce who was a bully. I mean he bothered everybody and I had to figure out a way to challenge this guy. I had a friend in the dorm named Earl who was smacked real hard by Bruce one day and I witnessed it. The staff allowed them to have a one on one fight. It was a good battle except I felt Bruce edged him out a little bit on points. However, I got to see his skills and deep down inside, I believed I could beat Bruce so I just kept waiting for him to try me.

One Saturday evening, we were in the closet getting out clothes to wear, and he suddenly bumped me. I reacted by shouting at him that he should try me like he tried everybody else. Bruce would go around sneaking punches on people, which we called "snuffing", and I wanted to be snuffed by him. I had the audacity to scream at him, and then bend down in front of him to pick up a towel. He delivered an upper cut that just grazed my chin, and as I proceeded to defend myself, the staff broke it up and locked me in my cell for the rest of the night.

Bruce was allowed to remain out of his cell, which I felt showed favoritism. He was laughing and talking crap outside the dorm while I was locked in my cell.

The next morning, I caught him by the closet and said, "What's up?" just before snuffing him back with a nice blow to the jaw. Before Bruce could return any blows, the staff came and broke the fight up. They told us they were going to tell the night staff to let us have a one on one that night so that we could handle this grudge. Everybody was anticipating the match between us that night. I was waiting to prove to the whole dorm I was the tougher guy, but before I could do that, Bruce was released when he went to court that day. I was disappointed because I'd been ready for battle.

* * *

Back in 1979, I was afraid of the older guys in the neighborhood, so they had an edge on beating me up. But when I would fight guys my own age, I would win. We had a lot of smack boxing competitions growing up in the projects which turned me into a bully when I was in public school. I went to P.S. 270, a school right across the street from my project building. Everyday, I used to make the kids bring me at least fifty-cents. There was this guy named Bryant, and I would smack him upside his head and demand he bring me money or else. I would chase guys home for not bringing me my money. I had a good number of fights while growing up.

I used to walk around saying I was a fighter with a twenty and five record as a street fighter. At the time, I was only ten, and becoming a boxer was the furthest thing from my mind. A career was the last thing a kid from the ghetto was thinking about. It's ironic that I became a boxer after all that fighting and bullying. And I even kept a street fight record!! Who knew? It's like God already had it planned. "Divine Intervention" as they say. That's the only way I can put two and two together and figure out how I linked up with the sport of boxing. Who would have ever thought that boxing would be what saved my life?

I also used to bother the girls in my school. They were very afraid of me because they thought I was crazy or retarded. I used to start trouble with people for no apparent reason. Sometimes I would smack students on the back of the neck as they waited in line for chow. Other times I used to curse at the teachers and throw chairs down the hallways and in the class rooms when I got agitated by a student or a teacher. This one girl I kept bothering named Renee, who was nine, had had enough. She told her father, who was a police officer and he came to school screaming and yelling that he would lock me up. He was a very scary looking man. After that, I never bothered her again or any of the other girls at school.

When I was eleven, Erving, who was ten, was placed in a Special Education class in PS 270. It looked cool, seeing him and the other students having fun playing in the yard and cafeteria while we were in the classroom doing academic work. Erving had gotten so bad they had to transfer him to a 600 school where he would get special attention. At first he was placed in Special Education in public school P.S. 270 but he got more violent so they transferred him to a more supervised school.

He used to get taken to school on a yellow school bus everyday. I thought to myself, "Wow, that's cool. He gets to be taken to school everyday". I wanted to be taken to school on that bus too. It seemed like they had freedom to do what they wanted to do in school, and I wanted that same privilege. So I intensified my bad behavior in school so that I could be placed in Special Ed as well. I tell you, when I think back now, I see how ridiculous I was because that kind of education sucked.

My mother couldn't handle me back then because I was a bad ass kid who didn't listen and did what I wanted to do. She had a pretty good job working at Chase Manhattan Bank, but they fired her for taking too many days off because of me. She would have to come back and forth to school due to the trouble I kept getting into fighting and cursing out the teachers.

I made life much harder for my mother because she wasn't making the money she used to make. In fact, she never got another job like that one ever again in her entire life. She had to resort to welfare for almost a decade. She had her own problems to overcome which enabled me to do what I wanted to do. Mentally and physically I was lost and living in a triple state of darkness. I stayed high off of weed, drank 40 ounces of Old English on a regular basis and always kept a pack of Newport cigarettes handy.

CHAPTER 3: GREAT VALLEY

After being in Spofford for three months, it was time for me to be placed upstate. They put a couple of us with shackles on our hands and feet, like we were some kind of murderers and placed us in a van to take us to our destinations. Everybody went to different facilities. I was driven all the way to Buffalo, New York with a carton of Newport cigarettes, and a one year bid ahead of me.

When I inhaled the smoke from my first Newport after three months of smoking Kool Lights at Spofford, it tasted so good. But when I got to Great Valley, I was told one of the rules was no smoking, which was a blessing in disguise, because I was able to kick the habit for good. I mean after all, I was only thirteen years old.

The staff at Great Valley did, however, allow me to smoke my last cigarette in the office as they read the rules to me. The first rule was to follow staff instructions twenty-four hours a day, seven days a week. The second rule was that I had to participate in group sessions every day. The third rule was no cussing, and the fourth rule was no smoking.

Here I was in this strange place, in a small town in upstate New York, which was seventy-five miles from Buffalo, New York. The place was in the mountains, up on a tall hill. It was a long green building about a block long, with two buildings on each side, about 75 to100 feet apart from one another.

This was an all boys camp, ranging in ages from nine to fifteen years old. At thirteen, I had to live with white and Hispanic people for the first time. There was a lot of tension and disputes among some of the kids, but we had to learn to live with each other. We were introduced into a world I'd never imagined. We were taught how to play golf and even got to meet the legendary Jack Nicklaus, a stone redneck-looking guy. He had a pure white, wealthy-looking face with freckles on it and red colored hair and blue eyes. He was wearing a golf outfit. He was a very pleasant person and smiled as he gave the crew golf instructions. We played golf in the summer, and went skiing in the winter. We were daredevils that weren't afraid to ride down any mountain.

One day I was riding down this big professional slope called Firecracker and lost control. Before I knew it, I had collided into the head counselor, Terry and his girlfriend. I knocked both of them down the hill and rolled over his petite girlfriend. Joe, another staff member, burst out laughing. Terry had this aggravated look on his face. But he knew from the look on my face, I didn't mean it and that the accident was unavoidable. His girlfriend just stared at me with those big blue eyes. I wasn't sure if it was a look of anger or whether she understood that it was an accident.

Terry just said, "Mitch, you have to be more careful next time when people are on the slopes."

And he was right, because I hit them really hard, and his girlfriend could've gotten hurt. I agreed and strapped back up and continued on my journey.

The camp's Great Skiing Program was free to us because the counselors had made a deal with the company that we would clean up the golf course before golf season, and the slopes before skiing season.

We were able to express our feelings, and learned how to share our emotions with each other. We also learned how to understand each other's race and culture and solve difficult problems. For example, a lot of the young blacks and Hispanics had problems with illiteracy and stealing. The Hispanics were weary people who seemed to always tell on people. I believed a lot of Hispanic people were undercover racists and I don't know if they hate, fear or are just jealous of black people. It's strange how they acted anti-social towards us the way white folks did but yet they grew up and lived in the same neighborhoods with us. However, a lot of them are very religious. The white boys were the brainy cats but had tendencies of being homosexuals. For some reason, white men were the ones up there participating in homosexuality more than any other race that I was aware of. I knew of several white men who were involved in this but I didn't know of any African-Americans or Hispanics, not to say that there weren't any. If so, they hid it well.

White guys also felt like they were more superior than other races. You could tell by the way they acted and how they spoke to us. They always had this authoritative attitude, poking their chests out and pointing their chins upward. As a thirteen year old, white men appeared weird and strange to me. They were totally different people whom I had not experienced before. The only thing that I knew about them was what I was taught: white men were slave masters who didn't respect black men.

Being at Great Valley, I was able to learn a lot about the white man's culture and their ways of thinking. One thing was some of their tastes in food. They did weird things, like eating jelly chicken sandwiches. I actually saw a white guy make a jelly sandwich then put some baked chicken inside the sandwich and then proceed to eat it just like that! I also saw a white boy put an entire peanut butter and jelly sandwich inside of a glass of milk and then chow down. To some of the white kids, this was all normal but to me it was madness. And it wasn't just me. Sometimes black kids and white kids would get into debates and arguments about each other's cultural habits. There was this one guy named Billy that I used to have side verbal battles with. Bill was this fat kid, weighing about 250 lbs at the age of 12. He had long hair with a long nose and was from Elmira, NY. We would debate and he would call me, "black monkey, jungle bunny, music playing nigger." Then I would retaliate by saying "you redneck, hillbilly, white trash cracker mother fucking devil." Billy and I joked with each other back and forth and accepted it peacefully. I guess it prepared us for the real world. We became very close from all the confinement with one another.

We even had to take showers with each other every day, twice a day, twelve kids in the shower at the same damn time. There were about four white boys, five black guys and three Hispanics It was madness. We were confined together like slaves on a slave ship packed together like sardines in a small can.

"The crew" would sit in a group and talk about all of our problems and come up with solutions. We started group sessions everyday by asking each other how their day was. We would then tell about our day. If we had a problem to discuss about someone's attitude, the crew would jump in that person's shit about the matter and try to change the situation. I learned to speak very well from all those group sessions. We had group everyday and we had to speak in a mature and polite manner to one another when solving problems.

One day in a group session, it was revealed that some kind of sex had taken place while we were cleaning up the slopes for skiing season. This white dude named Richard told a dude named Carl, "to bend over you fuckin' faggot. "He then proceeded to fuck him in the ass. This was shocking news to me. A few other dudes were even involved in the sexual activities. I never found out whether Richard and Carl got caught by a staff member, or whether Richard just wanted to confess, revealing that we had a gay person, Carl, among our group. Richard was that type of guy who did not care what people thought of him. And after what he did to Carl, I am guessing Richard was gay too. He was one of those brainy white boys that felt smarter than everyone else. All the black guys used to ask him for help in class.

Carl was tall and skinny and he did a lot of dumb shit. He ran away and went AWOL once every two months, and would get caught each time. Eventually, after five months, he successfully escaped. Before his final AWOL, he approached me during food service and offered to suck my dick, but I declined. I was thirteen years old and was at the masturbation point in my life when I was doing it often so I thought about considering it but then I said to myself, "Nah, That ain't my style. I ain't gay."I never even brought it up in group or told the staff about it. I just kept it a secret.

We did things at Great Valley that a black guy like me from the ghetto would never think about in a lifetime. We went ice fishing and salt water fishing, canoeing and camping. We also had cookouts featuring our catch of the day. We actually would walk on a frozen lake, drill a hole in the lake and fish through the hole. If the frozen lake gave out, that was our ass!! The fish we caught we put on the grill with the franks and burgers. We went canoeing and camping all summer on a weekly basis. We also built log cabins, played horseshoes, volleyball, basketball and football. We even had soccer matches against each other. We would divide into crews of twelve kids and play against each other. I became such a good athlete that I became the ping pong champion of our crew.

While in school, we had a music class, in which we mostly sang Billy Joel songs for almost a year straight. I guess the teacher was a big fan of Billy Joel, so those were the only songs we sang.

We were also very healthy kids, because they fed us all the right foods. We only ate baked and broiled foods, and we rarely ate junk food. When I first arrived at Great Valley, I was a fat kid, but after about three months, I was in terrific shape. I had developed a body like Evander Holyfield and Mike Tyson. Even though I was only thirteen, I was as solid as a rock. I had muscles bulging out everywhere and when I returned home, the girls in school eventually started calling me "muscle man".

In addition, we received good medical attention. During a routine examination, I was diagnosed with a back problem called scoliosis, which is a curvature of the spine. The doctors recommended I wear a brace. I was so scared and disappointed, that I laid in my bed and cried the whole day. The staff tried to comfort me by telling me not to worry, that it wasn't serious, but I didn't understand it and thought I'd be crippled for life. They called my mother to explain it to her, and she told me to just listen to the doctors, which I did.

I was put in a neck brace that made me stand up straight. They told me I'd have to wear it for two years. I had eight months remaining at Great Valley, and I wore it all the way until my time was up. When I was released, I continued to wear the back brace, only taking it off to shower or exercise.

When I went to my follow-up at Kings County Hospital in Brooklyn, and the doctors saw that after wearing the brace for over a year, there still wasn't any improvement, they told my mother that she should consider surgery. But my opinion is that they were giving us the brush off because my mother only had Medicaid and they did not want to make me another brace because it was expensive and insurance would not cover it. I questioned this because back at Great Valley, the doctors in Buffalo said I had to wear a brace for 2 years instead of one year. It seems to me that doctors in urban communities do not provide adequate medical care for minorities and thus they get short changed. This is why it is so important for our youths to become doctors. Bottom line, we need more black doctors.

I explained to them I wanted to be a champion boxer and they told me that if I had the surgery, I probably wouldn't be able to box again. They felt that since I was so young, and had a boxing career, it would be best to go for my dream and not risk tampering with my back. Now that I think back on it, if I had gotten the surgery and couldn't box, I can't say where or what I would be doing with my life right now.

* * *

Being in Great Valley made me a much better

person. My reading and writing improved greatly. I learned to speak well, socialize, interact with different races and personalities, and became a great athlete. I was a proud young man when I came home at thirteen years old.

Although the staff members were nice people, they still had some racial issues. There was a guy up there by the named of Sonny who was going around the camp calling white kids devils. Sonny was an inmate. When he was brought up into the group, they talked about why he was going around making remarks like that, and he stated that he was a five percenter, a righteous Muslim, and he believed in the Nation of Islam, and that Mitch Rose told him he was a part of the Nation also.

When some of the staff found out I was a part of the Nation of Islam, they had a fit. Even the ones I had a bond with were angry with me because they thought our friendship had been phony. But the fact is, I was just a young kid who was being a follower. When I was about eleven years old, the Five Percent Nation was becoming popular in urban communities. You had brothers going around the neighborhood trying to influence sisters and brothers to join. Teenagers started joining just to be a part of something. Some joined because of security and to be among a crew of brothers. Some joined because it was the style back then. And some joined because they truly believed it would better them as a person. As for me, I joined because the rest of my friends were joining so I went along for the ride. However, I did feel that some of the things they were preaching were true. They talked about the unjust treatment by whites toward blacks. This information was enticing and enlightening for me. I was named "Understanding

God Allah" by my teacher named "Sha King God Allah."

We were taught that eating pork was no good and drugs should not be used. We were discouraged from getting involved in negative activities but that did not stop us, we still got into illegal activity. A lot of the teachings weren't sincerely followed but it gave you a good sense of direction in life and I think it had a very positive affect on me. People tended to criticize and chastise the Nation of Islam. Some believe that it is a racist religion but I totally disagree and still do. I believe all religions are positive as long as they are helping individuals to be better people. Religion is not about hate. It's about help! People just tend to get offended whenever black folks speak out about being wronged. It's kind of like when Al Sharpton speaks out about a bias attack, police misconduct or a maneuver by the government that appears unjust. A lot of white people just don't like it when a black leader speaks out strongly on racial issues. I was like those black leaders - I wasn't afraid to speak out.

Joe, a staff member, was a mean looking redneck who didn't play. He knew karate and judo, and all the kids respected him because they were afraid of him. He knew our religion believed that the white man was the devil and couldn't be trusted. When we went to chow, and pork was served, Joe would make sure everybody ate all the food on their plate. He said we had to eat everything because it was a balanced meal, and if we didn't, we weren't following the rules. He would even walk around the tables to see if we ate all our pork. I hated to see Joe come to work on the days pork was served. Joe knew we were Muslims so he was just being malicious. It was wrong and illegal what he was doing but we were way upstate in the boondocks and nobody knew or cared. He just blatantly disrespected us and violated our rights.

There was this black staff member named John Gatton. He and another guy, who was a counselor, were the only black people in the small town near Great Valley. Whenever John was working, and pork was served, I would give him my serving to eat because he was a fat guy that liked to eat.

One day, Joe and John were working the same shift, and Joe saw me give John my pork and he had a fit. He began cursing and hollering at John about eating my food. John was confused because he didn't know they were forcing us to eat forbidden foods. He didn't understand the conspiracy, or know what it was all about. John had the whole staff mad at him because they thought he protected the kids who were part of the Nation of Islam. For a while, they ostracized him, because they felt he really didn't belong out there in their all white town anyway.

John lived out there with an ugly fat, white trash type of lady. The kind that none of the white men wanted: the forbidden one, the black sheep, the ugly duckling, the undesirable one. John and his wife did not seem to fit in. I used to hear other staff members say things like, "John, are you going home to your white trailer trash wife?" Knowing that he and only a few other blacks lived in a town of five thousand whites, it seemed to me like he just did not fit in. Nevertheless, he was a nice man, fair and reasonable.

* * *

My release date from Great Valley was January of 1984. My mother came and picked me up from Penn Station and we rode the A train to Brooklyn. Being away for fourteen months things seemed really different to me.

When I got off the train, walked across the street and went upstairs, the projects looked liked a strange place. I was right back in the same old dirty apartment where my mother and sisters lived. My room was empty, except for a broken down bed in the corner.

I thought to myself, where do I go from here? All of my homeboys were still locked up. I was the first one to come home. The only friends I had to look forward to were a 40 ounce of Old Gold and a bag of weed. I was a little bit older, and after jerking off for eleven months, I wanted some real sex. At the time, I was a month away from turning fourteen.

A couple of days after being home, I was hanging out in the lobby of my building, when this girl from school named Darlene tried to give me a play. I rejected her by telling her she was too young. I really didn't know what I was saying, because when I realized I had made a mistake by turning her down, it was too late. She gave up and changed her mind. It took me another two months to get my dick wet.

Eventually, I met a girl named Shinese while walking around a shopping area in downtown Brooklyn. I was near Albee Square Mall when I got up the nerve to speak to her. We stopped and talked for a while and exchanged numbers. Two days later, she called me and we set up a date for the next day. She came to my family's apartment with a copy of the movie Scarface. I was upstate when the movie came out so I had never seen it. Everybody was talking about it and I had told Shinese that I wanted to see it. We started watching the movie in the living room, kissing and talking throughout. I was enjoying it and told Shinese how much I appreciated her bringing it over. And to top it off, Michelle Pfieffer had my dick hard as a rock! It wasn't long before I made a move on Shinese.

I grabbed her hand and escorted her into my room where I laid her on the bed and unzipped her pants. When I saw that she wasn't resisting, I went for the finish and pulled down her pants and took off her sneakers. Her pink cotton panties with red hearts and polka dots were the last to come off of her before I literally tore my shirt off and eagerly pulled down my pants. Moments later, I dove in that pussy like I was going swimming. My dick felt like it melted inside her pussy. Within three or four strokes, I ejaculated. We both rolled over and within seconds, we took a nap. But before I closed my eyes, I said to myself, "mission accomplished."

Although I got laid, I got into trouble three days after I came home. Being young and black back then meant proving you were still tough. I had to prove to myself and others I was still bad and still a criminal that I wasn't scared straight from being incarcerated. So, I went and tried to do what I knew how to do, pickpocket and snatch gold chains.

I went back to our main spot, 14th Street and 8th Avenue. I was walking down the block looking for a victim, a good pocket to pick. I looked up and saw this one woman standing at the bus stop. I walked up behind her, touched the zipper on her pocketbook but I didn't have enough time to get into it because she got on the bus that had arrived. I let it go and proceeded up the block to a store called Mays to try to shoplift something. I opened the door and let the person behind me go in first, not knowing it was the detective that had been following me after he saw me trying to pickpocket that woman at the bus stop. As my arm held the door open, the detective slapped the cuffs on that same arm.

His name was Frank, and he was a cop with a fierce reputation for catching pick pockets. At the precinct, he was bragging and showing me a newspaper article the Post did on him about the amount of pick pocket suspects he'd apprehended. I recall this one black detective in the precinct asking me why was I trying to be a superhero. He told me that all the superheroes were dead; Bruce Lee, Elvis Presley and Jimmy Hendrix. What he was saying was that young black guys coming out of prison were still doing the same things instead of changing their lives. We were going back in the streets, trying to prove to our homies and people in the neighborhood we were still criminals. I never understood what he was talking about until years later.

I somehow found boxing after that encounter. It was about two weeks from my fourteenth birthday; I was still a juvenile. My mother came to pick me up from the Midtown Precinct. My court date was scheduled for a month later. Two weeks after that incident, I got into trouble again.

Eyes, one of the guys that had recruited me years ago, influenced me to pull a knife on this white guy in the train station. He told me the guy had a lot of money on him. The guy resisted and yelled for help. A black woman, who was working as a transit clerk, hollered on the microphone for us to leave the man along. We ran away with nothing. Two weeks later, as I was getting on the train to go downtown to do some more robbing, the transit worker recognized me and called the police. They stopped the train three stops later at Hoyt-Schermerhorn train station and arrested me and another guy named Anthony, who wasn't even with me just two weeks prior to this attempted robbery.

Since we were both juveniles, our mothers had to come and get us out. My mother just said to me that I was sick and needed help. She didn't beat or argue with me anymore, she just let me be. Anthony told his mother he had nothing to do with it, and she believed him.

I discovered boxing by smoking weed and dancing to rap music. I was at home doing aerobics, dancing like Richard Simmons with my shadow on the wall, when somehow I started swinging and moving my head around. One hour of that gave me a very good workout, which made me anticipant another workout like that.

Everyday after that, I'd follow the same routine; I'd smoke some weed, and then do creative exercises while shadow boxing. It looked so fascinating to see my shadow with the beautiful, sculptured body I had developed at Great Valley.

Age 13 at Great Valley with fresh leather pants and Adidas

CHAPTER 4: SCHOOL DAYS

A month later in February 1984, it was time for me to go to court to face one of the two cases. When I walked into the court, and the judge saw that I had just came home, he remanded me back to Spofford. I was right back behind bars, and I hadn't even been home for a solid month. I sat looking out the window, crying and wondering, what the hell was I doing back in here?

After being at Spofford for thirty days, it was time for me to go back to court. Being young and dumb, I decided to take the case to trial and blew it. The judge was now ready to render a sentence. In Family Court, which is different from Criminal Court, they make decisions right on the spot, whether or not you want to cop a plea or go to trial.

The judge asked me, "Young man, do you have anything to say before I sentence you?"

I stood looking at the judge. Being at Great Valley had taught me how to speak like a nerd and an Uncle Tom type of guy, and that's what saved my ass from being sent away again. I opened my mouth and told the judge how sorry I was, and that I could become a better person, that people underestimated my abilities. The judge was so impressed that he released me, but he told me that he didn't know what the judge in my other still pending case would do.

A couple weeks later, it was time to face that case. I tried to take that one to trial as well and lost. The man didn't remember me until I tried to take my gold tooth out, which was the only thing he remembered about me.

When the judge began deciding on my

punishment, I stared and looked directly into his eyes and said, "Your Honor, please give me one more chance. I know I can do better and I will. "

He looked directly into my eyes and said, "I believe you're sincere young man, and that you can change, so I'm going to extend your aftercare probation. "

Once again, I was a free man.

Although I continued my wave of crime, I took it easy after I turned sixteen because I knew that I would have a criminal record for life and end up in a more serious court such as the Supreme Court. A lot of people in the neighborhood were conditioned to think that it was okay to get caught as an adult at least once because they would only get probation. This was a stupid way of thinking but was part of hood tradition.

The only thing that saved my life and freedom was my mother. She opted to give me an allowance of fifty dollars a week, which was a lot for a sixteen-year old back then. I didn't have rent to pay and I didn't have any real responsibilities other than staying out of jail. I had my brew and weed money, with a little left over for "my girl" money. I was straight. My mother never had much money but even with some of the welfare money she had she would give it to me to stay out of trouble.

I was attending a school called Rough Child. It was a junior high school that went to the 9th grade. (I got left back in the third grade.) I was placed back in Special Ed where I left off fourteen months ago. It was a cool school with a lot of girls and people I remembered from when I was at PS 20. I thought I was the coolest dude in the school because I had a lot of fresh gear to wear. I even had a couple of gold chains and rings I wore that I had snatched off people in Midtown.

I met one of my first girlfriends in that school while hanging out in the hallways. Her name was Karen. She was this fine dark-skinned chick that had a real nice figure for a 14-year-old. She reminded me of Angela Bassett. We only dated for a short time because I thought I was too cool and fly for her.

One day, I was in the hallway talking to this other girl and Karen walked by and saw me talking to the girl. She looked at me like her heart had dropped into her stomach but I was determined to get this other girl's phone number. She was this slim Spanish mami named Diane. Diane gave me her number right on the spot.

Later that day when I walked into the cafeteria, Karen was sitting at a table looking at me, crying. I knew she wanted me to come over and apologize, but I continued with my macho attitude. I just looked at her in the face and laughed. Her friends surrounded her, trying to comfort her with sympathy and compassion.

Karen and I had sex only two times. The first time, she stated that she was a virgin. I really didn't believe her, although her pussy was very tight. At the time I didn't care, because I was a wild and crazy kid that walked around school high off weed and beer. As for me wanting to hook up with Diane, it was just a freak thing. I dumped her after two or three fucks too. She was a very religious girl and always talked about God and Jesus. I was not trying to hear that bullshit back then. I just wanted some sex so I had to get away from her real quick.

* * *

Meanwhile, I was still practicing my shadow boxing and dreaming of becoming a boxer. I was in the school hallway shadow boxing when two school safety officers came and told me I shouldn't be hanging in the hallways. I shouted at them, "You can't tell me what to do!"

When I stepped into a boxing stance, one of the officers, who happened to know karate, challenged me. He kicked me in the balls and rushed me with his walkie-talkie, banging me all upside my head. I landed on the floor, and when I looked up, guess who I saw - Karen. I guess it was sweet revenge for her.

I had suffered my first defeat as a street fighter since I had started practicing boxing aerobics. The officers took me in a room and tried to intimidate me. The officer, knowing he had gotten the best shot, knew he had me kind of nervous. I went home bruised up and angry. That night, I must've shadowed boxed for about two hours straight.

I came to school the next day with a Bruce Lee sweatsuit on, the yellow and black one he wore in the movie "Enter The Dragon," looking for a rematch and revenge. I walked into the lobby and approached the sergeant at the desk. I asked him for the officer that had assaulted me yesterday, and was told he'd been transferred to another school, so I was never able to get my revenge.

I eventually graduated from Rough Child Junior High School in June of 1985 and somehow landed in Clara Barton High School. Even though my mother was trying to get me back into mainstream classes, I was still placed in Special Education. It was a helluva school that had something like a hundred boys to a thousand girls. I was in heaven. I knew that I was the flyest brother in school, because my wardrobe was awesome. I had shoplifted all kinds of clothes; Adidas, Ralph Lauren, you name the brand, I had them. I also had crazy gold chains, diamonds and pearls.

My school was in a neighborhood in Flatbush with a lot of Jamaican and Caribbean hoodlums that used to stare me down, clocking my jewelry after school. I started carrying a gun in my backpack. One afternoon, I came outside when school was over and these Jamaicans, who were hanging out in Prospect Heights High School across the street, started staring at me. I knew they wanted to rob me of my jewelry, but I had heart. I wasn't afraid and I stared right back at them before walking off.

They eventually caught me off guard, which happened to be on the day I wasn't carrying my gun. They jumped me right in front of the school while the cops were right down the block in their car. One guy jumped on my neck and held on tight. Even though he was a skinny dude, I couldn't shake him off. I fell to the ground looking helpless as the cops sat in their car parked on the corner just staring at us.

I began to wonder, when are these guys going to help me?

Finally they pulled up and spoke on the horn radio, "Alright guys, break it up!" I figured they were two lazy, fat ass black cops, who didn't care if we beat the shit out of each other because they are used to seeing stuff like that in the hood. They never even got out the car to see if I was alright.

I screamed to them, "I want to file a police report!"

Two white detectives came on the scene to investigate things. They took me for a ride to finger these guys. I saw them out there and pointed them out to the cops. They were standing right around the corner from the school on Carroll and Franklin Avenue. They got locked up, but I didn't press charges, I just wanted them to feel it for that moment. That was something I got from Tarzan and Eyes. They would rob anybody, but if you robbed them, they'd run straight to the cops.

After that incident, I no longer felt safe in that neighborhood. The school thought it was best that I get transferred, and I agreed, but only on one condition. I wanted to get mainstreamed into regular classes and they agreed. In April of 1986, I began attending Sara J. Hale High School. This was the second high school that I attended. I was getting the opportunity for a new start and a new outlook on life. I was back on my side of town, and I planned on staying there, Bed-Stuy do or die. The school was less disciplined and it was easier to get a diploma. I was seventeen years old and had graduated to another form of robbery called digging. I began to blow up. I was getting fresher and fresher, trying to be the number one man in school.

I saw this guy with a Run DMC chain on and it looked so fly, I knew I had to get me one too. Then I saw this young dude in school driving a car that was so fly, I told myself I had to get me a car like that.

My friend, Darryl, Craig's older brother, took me to buy my first car, which was a Cutlass Sierra. I dressed it up how the Puerto Ricans dressed up their Cutlass', with the wheels in the back raised up and the front low. I had a weird way of thinking, because no black guys really rode in cars like that, just Spanish dudes. I used to park in front of the school and show off by stepping out of my car with my book bag slung over my shoulder. When I strolled up the steps, all the girls would become mesmerized. I even saw the girl, who would eventually be my wife watching me. I felt like the coolest man on the planet.

I was this handsome young guy, with a big gold chain on walking through the cafeteria looking like LL Cool J. I was in great shape, with a great physique. I would hear the girls in the background, oohing and aahing, saying, "Look at that guy's muscles".

* * *

I was in my fourth year as a boxer. Just because you don't have any fights, it does not mean that you are not a boxer. I trained and sparred all kinds of guys in the gym. I was preparing and perfecting my skills. Eventually, it was time to test what I have been practicing all those years. I remember the first day I started. The gym was called Bedstuy Boxing Association. I walked into the gym after six months of shadow boxing in my house. I was in the mirror at the gym shadow boxing, practicing my craft, when this trainer named Johnny Boy came up to me and said, "Hey son, you want to be a fighter?"

Excitedly, I said, "Yeah."

I had been waiting for someone to come and help me out, but I didn't know where to start. Johnny Boy showed me how. He was a fair trainer, but there were a lot of things he didn't know, which I believe had a lot to do with me not becoming the heavyweight champ of the world. I was also a screw up as well. I smoked and drank most of my career

and had a good amount of girlfriends. I was also still hustling and robbing for a living. I guess that caused me to have a lot of bad luck in my boxing career.
Back then I used to go to the gym high off weed. I would get a good creative workout high. I'd even sparred high, busting my sparring partners up pretty bad. Then I'd go to Midtown looking for my next victim.

Rahiem, Erving, Melvin, and a couple of other cats and I were in Midtown, when we saw some dudes digging in people's pants pockets as they walked down the block. They didn't waste time trying to sneak their wallet out their pants, they just snatched the whole pocket out and had the guy's pockets looking like rabbit ears. These guys were from Harlem, and the rumor was that's where digging originated. We copied them and started digging too. Sometimes when digging, you would rip a guys pocket off or we would dig our whole hand into the suit pocket and pull out all of the money inside, sometimes to the point that even the change came out.

Digging was when you slid your hand into someone's front pocket and very precisely grabbed the money out of the pocket and ran. Diggers were very bold and almost dug anybody. I saw dudes dig a blind man. I even saw a digger dig a man in a wheel chair. Diggers took chances, sometimes digging people a block from the police station.

We would travel four or five guys deep, looking for money prints, which was pockets that appeared to have the measurement of money, in mostly white guys pockets, even though we would occasionally dig a black or Hispanic guy, the majority were white guys, because they were the ones that carried the real money. A lot of them sometimes would have over four thousand dollars in their pockets and the majority wouldn't put up much resistance. White businessmen carried money like that all of the time. They would have two thousand, fifteen hundred, three thousand and much more. They would just stand there shouting, "you fuckin' nigga!" as we ran away. Very rarely did the white guys chase after us, but a black or Hispanic guy would start screaming and chasing us all over Midtown, so we tried to avoid them whenever possible.

Most of the time I was the lookout, while the guys I was with did the digging. My job was to stop the superhero that tried to get involved and help the victim. This was our job. This was what we did mostly every weekend. Sometimes we worked for the three card monty guys being their lookout man for the police. Sometimes we sold tickets for the scalpers outside in front of Madison Square Garden. We learned all types of hustles while in Midtown. We didn't consider ourselves violent criminals, just daredevils that took chances.

There wasn't a block in Midtown that we wouldn't go down; 59th Street, 14th Street, 42th Street Times Square. But Canal Street in Chinatown was the most daring spot to play, because Chinese people had a lot of heart, they'd chase us for blocks.

One day Black, Huck, Rahiem, two other guys and I were on Canal Street and someone dug a pocket. Suddenly, Chinese guys started coming from everywhere. I wanted to stay and fight, but everyone else started running, so I yelled, "Come on guys, let's stay and fight! There are only three guys!"

Black shouted, "You crazy man, it's a lot of them!"

So I had no choice but to run too. We ran

down the block toward the train station, with the Chinese guys still on our heels. When we got to the entrance to the train station, two chubby cops were slowly walking down the steps. We busted through them, pushing them out the way to get down the steps. We even knocked over their coffee and donuts to get away from those guys. Now we had the cops and the Chinese guys chasing us.

We jumped the turnstile, ran down the steps that led to the tunnel where the trains were. The cops and Chinese guys were still behind us, so I jumped on the tracks and hid under the platform.

Some white lady on the other side of the platform, who didn't have anything to do with the situation, yelled out, "He's under there!"

One of the cops looked at her and asked, "Where?"

She pointed to where I was hiding and said, "Under there, right under there. " But the cops continued to follow the path of the other guys running down the platform and onto the tracks. I popped up, gave the white lady the finger and went back up the steps where I ran into two of the Chinese guys that had been chasing us. One of the guys had a two by four, which he swung at me. I dipped and hit him with a left-right combination, and when the other guy saw the combination, he hesitated.

The conductor screamed into the microphone, the same way that lady did back when me and Eyes were trying to rob that man, "Leave that man alone!"

When I jumped over the turnstile, I saw a gated entrance that was closed, but the keys were hanging in the lock. I opened it and quickly locked it back, leaving the two Chinese guys on the other side of the gate. They stood banging on the gate with the two by four. I spit at them, turned and ran back down the platform to the other side, only to run into the same white lady that was yelling out my hiding spot earlier. She started yelling to the cops again, and this time, they came running. I just gave up. The cops grabbed me and took me to the precinct that was stationed right inside the train station. They held me there while they tried to find a victim. I was released later that day because there was no plaintiff. Everybody else had gotten away by running through the train tunnel. One thing I can say is back in those days we believed white people especially loved snitching on black people. As far as we were concerned, we thought most white people were the police in some form or another.

With mother at graduation 1987

Graduation picture 1987

Chillin at Sarah J Hale H.S. with girls

My first car, a Cutlass Sierra

CHAPTER 5: MIDTOWN DIGGERS

We had young guys in the neighborhood that wanted to become diggers, like it was some kind of career or something. They used to come up to me, like I was a digging manager. That's how I recruited Lee. Lee, who was thirteen at the time, came up to me while I was standing on Classon Avenue, and asked me if he could make some money because he heard about my reputation in Midtown. Lee was a little dirty kid with brown teeth, nappy hair and dirty clothes. I felt bad for him, but figured I might as well make some money off him. He didn't have anything to lose.

I named him Black, because he was a dark skinned brother. He had a lot of courage in Midtown. When I told him to "get that," whether it was a gold chain or fat pocket, with a lot of money, he'd get it.

The projects were like a negative magnet. Innocent kids were being sucked into a lifestyle of crime and drugs, because of the lucrative things they saw that the other guys had in the hood.

Two weeks later, I recruited this other guy named, Kay-Kay. I named him K-Love, because he was a gentle giant that loved to eat cakes and potato chips. He was also thirteen. He was a real sloppy guy, and when he dug a pocket, he would knock people down, run over old ladies, do whatever it took to get away.

Rahiem, Divine, Erving, and a couple of other guys, would dig pockets while I was the lookout and the bodyguard. I used to tell these guys I handled security and I thought I did a pretty good job because none of them got caught when they were with me.

Even though I wasn't doing any of the digging, I did look out for their best interest. I was sincere when it came down to stopping a hero and I observed the areas we played to make sure no detectives were following us. I also kept train tokens. We called them getaway tokens in Midtown just in case somebody forgot theirs, and most of them did. These guys didn't care who they robbed, nor did they pay attention to what was going on around them. They were more eager to dig somebody, and I used that to my advantage. They also stayed broke because they didn't know how to save money. I had learned to stretch money from when my mother used to give me allowance to stay out of trouble, so I knew how to make a hundred dollars last for about two weeks.

Don't get me wrong. Sometimes I would dig in a second if it was necessary. I felt that if I dug something, it would be just for me, or maybe I'd split it with one other person. I didn't believe in splitting up my money with four or five guys. I didn't feel it was worth it, plus I was very cautious because I still had a goal of becoming the heavyweight champion of the world. I didn't want to ruin my career because of crime in Midtown.

Out of all the guys I used to hang out with, I was the only one that always got away. I quit the game of digging first and was the only one that didn't catch a felony conviction or do time in jail. As we grew older, it seemed like they had a lot of animosity toward me because of my elusiveness back in Midtown.

Back when we were in Midtown I think the reason I used to get away more than those guys was because of my experience out there and my athletic abilities. I used to train in the morning for our pick pocket excursions to Midtown by jogging about three or four miles a day, so that I could be tuned and alert. I thought I was untouchable inside and outside the ring. I practiced defense constantly, and even to this date, it's hard to hit me in the ring. This one boxer named Ernest, who was my sparring partner, used to say I had one of the best defenses in boxing.

It's like we turned Midtown into some kind of art or something, because damn near all the guys in LaFayette Gardens started digging pockets. They kept hearing about the bonuses we were taking in Midtown. I would brag when I took a bonus, or when my crew took a brick, which is a wad of money that was a thousand dollars or more. If we took three thousand, we'd say it was about five. If we took five, we'd say it was eight. All of this was to impress and degrade others. It wasn't Midtown if we didn't hype it up. The new guys that were coming out didn't have any real knowledge about Midtown, they just dug a pocket anywhere or anytime without staking the place out first. That's why a lot of them didn't last too long and went to jail within a week or a month.

They didn't examine the person they chose to dig. They just went after anybody and most of the time if you dug a young guy who was in good shape, he would give you a run for your money and chase you for blocks possibly until he ran you into a cop. Therefore, smart diggers would try to avoid people like that. However, sometimes they would take a chance if the pocket looked fat with a bonus that we felt was worth the risk. Usually, though they would pick on middle age men or senior citizens. Fat people who ran slow were also targets or maybe a guy with a limp who was handicapped.

I can't estimate exactly how many diggers there were, but I believe there were about a hundred out there in Midtown. I used to see about ten when my crew and I would be out there. I believe about at least one hundred people got their pockets dug on a monthly basis in Midtown.

My theory is that is why a lot of white people in New York City are so racist and angry at young black youths. They would get their pockets dug right in front of their wives and kids. It had to be embarrassing, because I would look at some of their faces after they were dug, and they would turn red, some even looked like they wanted to cry. When the guys got through with digging them in Midtown, you were able to see the true definition of a racist, like Michael Richards aka Kramer from "Seinfield" acted when they booed his jokes.

After a while, things started to really get out of hand and I didn't like what I was seeing. I recall K. Love digging a man one day in Midtown so rough by dragging him about 20 feet standing up trying desperately to get the money out of his pocket until he ripped the man's whole pants leg off. K. Love just ran. I felt bad for the man so I went over to the old man and asked him if he was okay. Then I acted like I was chasing after K. Love and shouting "Hey, come back with that man's money!" We got away and split up the money, but I screamed at K. Love, telling him he had to be more careful when digging. He asked me was I crazy or something. No, I wasn't crazy but from my standpoint, I saw it like this: I was out to make money. I did not want to hurt anybody and I did not want an assault charge, especially for a robbery.

A couple of weeks later, I was out in midtown and a couple of other guys and I dug a man on the steps of the train station. The man lost his balance and was falling down the steps but I reached out and caught him in the air like Elliott Ness did in the movie "The Godfather", when he caught the baby carriage as it was tumbling down the steps. I stood the man back up and he looked at me like he was in shock. Then we darted down the steps and jumped the turnstile and hopped on the A train and went home. Yes, we were robbing folks but my main mission was always to steal money smoothly without anyone getting hurt.

When we were digging, sometimes we would have a victim's whole wallet with all of their ID in it, and my boys would just throw it on the ground. I used to feel so bad for the person that I would pick up the wallet and put it in a bag and mail it back to the person. The fellas used to think I was stupid, but I felt that it was a terrible thing for a person to lose all of their ID because of idiots like us. That was just me. I was just a kind hearted person. I didn't like what we were doing to people but I needed money. I had to survive.

One month later, I heard about two diggers, Pig and Drac from Brownsville that had caught a body. They allegedly dug a man by the platform in the train station while a train was coming. The old man lost his balance and fell near the tracks busted his head and died. The police were looking for Pig but before they could catch him he was murdered in Cypress Hills Projects. His partner Drac was the only one apprehended. He was tried and convicted and was sentenced to 25 years to life. The scary part about it was that the word on the streets from the Midtown society was that Drac did not have anything to do with the crime. He just happened to be in the wrong place at the wrong time, and facing an all white jury is like suicide, so the wrap got pinned on him. Then it was alleged later that a guy named Ty from around East New York confessed to the robbery and tried to free Drac but the system did not accept his plea. There was also a guy named Ness who used to dig so many pockets in Midtown that he used to go to the Empire Skating Rink to impress the ladies by burning one hundred dollar bills in front of them. One day he dug a pocket in Midtown, got chased into the train tunnel while trying to get away from five O and slipped and fell onto the third rail. He was electrocuted and died right there on the tracks.

After that, some diggers from around LaFayette Gardens were involved with an incident that made the front page of the Daily News. A tourist captured a picture on his camera of about five of them in action. Midtown South police came and picked up every one of them and locked them up. After hearing about those incidents, and seeing the paper, I was ready to throw in the towel. Things in Midtown started getting more violent and more serious than I had anticipated. I started hearing about a lot of dudes doing three or four year bids for digging. It became too risky and not worth it. Dudes around the way would ask me to go out and I'd tell them, "No, I'm finished with that life. There's gotta be a better way. "

* * *

Racism is a very ugly thing. I believed back then digging was a form of racism, because when most of us dug pockets, we were fueled with anger. Sometimes we'd rip a white man's whole pants leg off his body, believing he had a lot of slave trade money in them. A lot of those white guys were corrupt businessmen who were racist bloodsuckers of the poor. Anyway, that's what we believed back then.

Even though it didn't give us the right to rob them, it was our poisonous way of thinking.

Black people had this belief that all white people had money. They didn't understand their race, just like white people didn't understand our race. I believed that was always going to be a problem between us because we didn't live among each other. When I was in Great Valley, we had to learn to eat, sleep, shit and just generally understand each other's culture. We had to have dinner at the same table with each other. We lived together, shared bunk beds and shared bathrooms. It didn't matter whether a white guy was gay or a former skinhead or that a black guy couldn't read or had an attitude problem, we had to learn to live with each other. That's why today I can get along with all people and don't feel any prejudice around them. Unfortunately, that's not the case for the majority of the people on this planet.

I believe that people who are racist should keep it to themselves because that's a very evil way to be. Whoever is racist should be isolated into their own communities because they are an imminent danger to our society and capable of causing serious destruction to someone's life. Racists may set you up and falsely accuse you of something or target you for attack because of your race. They could kill you maliciously while driving and say it was an accident or convict you of a crime when you're innocent, or just bust you upside your head while no one's looking.

With this negative way of thinking, it made youths such as myself believe there was no hope for a black man in America. That's why we continued our life of hustling and wave of crime.

Digging days

Hanging with Joe and Black

CHAPTER 6: DRUG GAME

I had a friend named Craig that lived in my building, who told me that selling drugs was the best way to make money and he had a plan on how to get started. This was in 1987. Now Craig did not grow up the way me and my boys grew up. He came up in Catholic school and his mother and father were always there for him. He had parents that disciplined him and gave him an allowance until he was about eighteen years old. He used to walk me, Rahiem and Erving to the train station, mostly every morning when we were headed to Midtown to do our thing. He would never come with us. He'd just tell us to be careful while giving us a look of hopelessness, knowing we were heading for self-destruction.

In 1987, he was the one who got me started in the drug trade. Craig started trying to sell drugs at an older age than we started doing crime. He was 21 years old. We put a hundred dollars together and bought our first package of crack. We bought two eight balls, which consisted of three and a half grams apiece for a total of seven grams.

We bottled up the crack in vials, and stood in the back of our building under a tree and waited for addicts to come by. Coincidently, there was a crack spot right across the street from our building on Classon Avenue, so we were able to intercept the spot's regular customers. The drug dealer that owned the spot wasn't a violent type guy, so he really never tried to raise war. He did, however, holla at Craig one day, trying to scare him away. But when I saw him and stared him down with a violent look, he backed down like he was afraid of me and the way I looked. I was the type of guy that you could tell was ready for war, although I was as scared as he was, but I kept my cool. Besides, this guy had been at that spot for a couple of years already, so his pockets were fat. It was time for mine to get fat too.

Knowing that we were standing outside, most of the crackheads felt it was better to buy from us then to go into the stairwell, risking getting cornered by the police. Besides, they knew us from the neighborhood, so they preferred to give the business to us instead of a guy that wasn't even from around our way.

We used to buy from a guy named Dave that lived on Bedford Avenue. He used to sell us already cooked up crack, and the addicts loved it. Our clientele started growing fast. After we built our quantity up to about ten eight balls, we opted to go solo.

I was more aggressive and determined than Craig, and I had more time on my hands. Craig had a nine to five, so he sold drugs part-time, which gave me time to advance and make more money. Craig was also experimenting with crack. He'd lace his blunt with crack sprinkled in it. In the hood they called them woolers.

In 1987 things were really starting to get out of control in the neighborhood. Robberies went up, violence increased, and the neighborhood was becoming really unsafe. The tenants in the building started complaining about the increase of strange people entering the property. We had a lot of new faces hanging around our building. Addicts were also loitering around. Parents started becoming afraid to come outside to go back and forth to work.

Word got back to Craig's mother that he was

involved with crack and dealing in the neighborhood. She confronted him and told him to quit or get out of her apartment. He came and told me he was finished with dealing, which meant I had the whole projects to myself. Craig even became an occasional customer of mine. Yes, Craig got high off of his own supply. In fact, he was already using before we started selling. That's how he knew that selling drugs was a money maker.

My mother was never able to control me, so she pretty such stayed out of my way. In my room, I bottled up my crack, smoked, drank and fucked on a regular. I didn't think about the possibility of my mother getting evicted or our apartment getting raided, because I was living fast in a lost world.

Everyday I'd hustle in the back of the projects by myself. I would carry about fifty crack vials in my pockets. They'd last about an hour, then I'd have to run back upstairs and get more. Crack was the fastest product I ever saw sold. They sold like all-star basketball tickets, and I became well respected by the crackheads because I was a generous drug dealer. I would give them credit when they didn't have money, or I'd give them shorts when they couldn't scramble up the whole three or five dollars. I sold nickels and trays of crack. Most of the crackheads worshipped me like I was a god, making me feel like a celebrity or superhero.

My name started spreading around the neighborhood fast, even to the police. Parents and neighborhood snitches were giving up tips on me. Some of my customers would come back and tell me about information they heard around the way. They looked up to me, because even though I was a drug dealer, they knew I was a decent person.

After a few months of pumping crack, things started heating up. Undercover cops were staking out the building I lived in and people started getting arrested for all types of crimes. The parents hated me and believed I was a bad influence and an evil man. I could feel the tension and I saw the hate in some of their eyes. It was time for me to fall back. Besides, my connections were getting busted all the time, and it was difficult for me to get more crack regularly. My business started falling apart so by the end of 1987, I just stopped selling and laid low with the savings I had accumulated.

Three months later, this young guy around the neighborhood named Wise came up to me and asked if he could sell drugs for me. He told me how he admired the way me and my crew enjoyed life and wore the best clothes and jewelry. I told him selling drugs wasn't a good life for him. I knew him to be a pretty good kid, who attended Catholic school and stayed out of trouble. But he was determined to go forward with the drug trade.

He tried to team up with this other guy in the neighborhood named Randy, aka Knowledge Born, Mr. Cee of Hot 97 younger brother. Once I saw Knowledge making power moves, I jumped right back into the game and partnered up with Wise. I put the packages together while he did the selling. We rose to the top like Neno Brown in New Jack City. Once again, I was on top of the food chain.

This was my second time around holding down the projects. I even bragged to people that I was the ambassador of the projects. I felt like Scarface. I had plenty of friends and girls hanging around me daily. Some days I tried to act like Scarface by sniffing coke from a pile on the table the way he did. I usually used drugs once every few weeks or so. A lot of young guys copied that scene, and that's probably how they got hooked on coke and crack.

Eventually Wise and I started smoking woolers together on a regular basis. Things, however, started to get out of control. I was sitting on a chain fence in the projects with a 40 of Old Gold, and said to myself, why am I always drinking and smoking? Am I an addict? That's the first time I realized that this thing was getting serious, so I decided to test myself and see if I could go without getting high.

After only three days, I was having cravings for crack, weed and brew. I was told that when an addict needed a fix, they started sweating, which is exactly what happened to me. I said to myself, no way, I can't go out like this. I'm nobody's crackhead. I refused to walk around dirty and skinny, looking to steal from my own people. I had seen a lot of my homeboys get really messed up off the stuff. They were stealing from their girlfriends, mother, and anybody else around them.

The drug game is an evil business, and there are six million ways to die from it. Making a lot of dirty money like that causes murderers and stick-up kids to watch you continuously. They would come around the projects five and six deep, and they all wore army fatigue coats and hoodies. By then, Wise and I had about six workers selling crack for us.

The armed bandits rushed one of the buildings in the back of the projects where four of my workers were hanging out and made them get on the floor. They ripped out their pockets and stripped them of all their valuables, including my crack. When they came and told me about the robbery, I became fed up with these intruders threatening my operation. It was now time to use the arsenal that I purchased while being in the drug business. I never really had to use them but it looked like it was coming to that point.

I put on my bulletproof vest, armed myself with two guns and gave a gun to Wise. He looked intimidated and scared because he hadn't been involved in anything like this before. I could tell he was reluctant and didn't want to go to war with those thugs, but I felt that I had no other choice. Besides, I had to show all my boys that I was a courageous leader. Although gunplay wasn't my style, I'd bust a gut if I had to. I wasn't a coward. Every time I went looking to go to war with those guys, they had already robbed somebody and vanished. Most of the time I hustled, I did not have problems with people. Nobody bothered me because I used to use psychological warfare by showing off my stash of weapons. I would show off my 45 caliber automatic, my nine millimeter and tec nine assault weapon to my workers and some of the brothers around the neighborhood. They would spread the word that I had a lot of dangerous weapons. That was my strategy. I did this because I understood how the community operated.

By this time, I had about seven workers selling crack for me. My name was growing so fast as the man running the drug trade at the L. G. projects. Different kids just kept coming to my building looking for me trying to get a job. I kept hiring people. I was hiring so many people that some guys would come first to get one two hundred dollar package, steal it from me, and never come back. This one guy named Easy from around the way was one of the last guys I was tolerating coming to con me out of a package. I knew his intention was just to swindle me. He came and told me that times were hard and that he needed a job and that he heard that I was the man.

I gave him a chance and the dude got me for a $200 package. I went looking for him and caught him in one of the project buildings I threw him up against the wall and put my . 38 Snub nose caliber up against his head and demanded my money back. I cocked my trigger back to try and intimidate him. He reacted by pushing my arm out of the way, then the gun went off and missed his head by about two inches. He then darted to the staircase and ran down the steps. I just stood in the hallway shocked about what happened. I was only trying to scare the guy to let him know that I wasn't a punk and at the same time I was letting out my frustrations about taking all of those losses. I almost killed a man for $200. This is when I really started contemplated about getting out of the drug trade. I had seen enough.

I continued to lose money. I passed one of my best workers a wooler and he started smoking. He passed the wooler to one of the other workers and he started smoking, and it went on and on, like a set of dominoes. Soon this included both workers and friends. Next thing I knew, four or five of my workers were smoking, and they didn't know how to control it like I thought I was doing. They started smoking whole packages and I started losing money. Eventually my business collapsed because I didn't have loyal workers anymore. The strongest ones lost respect for me because they thought I was cracked out too.

* * *

The potent crack I made I called "a strong molecule" because of how high a little of it made people. I used to cook it in a whistler and block the smoke from coming out the hole, so that no chemicals would be released. A whistler is a glass jar that is used to make coffee or tea. It whistles when the water is hot. I wanted it compressed into one powerful rock, so that when you took a pull, it would put you on the great space coaster. That's what I used to tell my customers. Crack had the whole projects running around like zombies, robbing and bashing people's heads in for more crack. Crack made people do crazy things and I saw some crazy, messed up stuff.

Things had gotten so bad during the crack era, that I used to see Hasidic Jews coming around the neighborhood driving away with crackheads to most likely commit a sex act or crime. I wasn't really sure what the deal was. I wasn't even sure whether or not they were the real Hasidic Jews or some impostors posing as Hasidic Jews. It just made me real suspicious and curious because a lot of those drug addicts were either HIV infected or contracted AIDS at an alarming rate in that era. I had three cousins, all sisters and brothers and all addicted to crack, and they had this one guy who dressed like a Hasidic Jew with the long beard, all black clothes and everything. The guy's appearance was nasty because he had constant rashes on his neck and arms. Every time I saw him, the rashes were there. He hung around my cousins all of the time. This guy used to be at family gatherings and parties with all black people. He pretended that he was not uncomfortable but I could tell that he was. I found it to be mind-boggling. Eventually, all three of my cousins contracted the virus, one after another. It made me wonder was it some kind of conspiracy by a group of guys posing as Hasidic Jews and spreading the AIDS virus in urban communities. I was so curious after my three cousins passed away that I went to investigate by interviewing a couple of current and former crackheads about what could have been going on. What I found out is that a lot of people believed that the people we were seeing were the real Hasidic Jews. People in the community believed that they were just out looking for fun and a cheap thrill like a lot of the other men were doing back then when decent women were getting hooked on crack. Although I thought the Hasidic Jews we were seeing were probably impostors, nobody else did. However, a few people in the community told me that these guys only wanted to pay $5 for sex acts, usually a blow job or even intercourse. I am sure that a lot of people in the neighborhood know what I am talking about and saw these suspicious acts as well on a regular basis. Eventually, these sightings and activities slowed down as minorities started getting AIDS at a faster rate. What I am talking about here are actual things that I witnessed in my neighborhood that I believe other people in the community are afraid to speak up about. Hopefully, whoever participated in this sexual open season era protected themselves to the fullest and did not become a victim of AIDS or some other life threatening disease because my three cousins were not as fortunate.

It is a weird episode to see a Hasidic man in his full religious outfit with a crackhead inside of his parked car, getting a blow job on a side block where drug users hangout. Eventually, I found out from a former crackhead friend of mine that those Jews were also smoking crack. They used to use crackhead women to purchase crack for them.

I was told a story by my friend Darryl who used to be on crack back in the early '90s, that one Labor Day holiday on the corner of Lincoln Place and Kingston Avenue in Brooklyn, a Hasidic Jew tried to purchase crack at the crack spot but the seller told him that he was not serving Jews on that day. He said that the product that he had left over was only for the minorities. Most likely the Jewish guy went and recruited a crackhead to buy the crack for him. Seeing this type of stuff made me wonder about a lot of things that go on in the hood.

For one, it made me think about all of the different places to eat ran by other nationalities in the neighborhood. For example, the numerous Chinese restaurants which served fried chicken wings and fried rice. Is it something in these foods that is causing an alarming rate of diabetes and high blood pressure in urban communities. And now, Asians are running the majority of the nail salons and people are getting infections from tools used for manicures and pedicures. Or are they maliciously not cleaning the equipment causing the spread of AIDS and other diseases in urban communities? And then you have the Arabs running all of the Kennedy Fried Chickens and delis making the turkey and cheese heroes. Could it be that they are doing something to these sandwiches and other food? I mean afterall, America is at war with their countries. In my opinion, African-Americans should spend more time eating in soul food restaurants. Some more unfortunate catastrophes are occurring all throughout the urban communities. Someone or some organization is distributing counterfeit trojan magnum condoms throughout the urban neighborhoods. Is this a conspiracy to eradicate Black Americans and who is responsible for this travesty? After all, Blacks are the most hated nationality in America surveys revealed. Could it be the Arabs or the Dominicans because they own the bodegas? Or could it be the White government who sell the products to the bodegas? I spoke with one local Arab bodega owner about this and he said, "Why would Muslims target Blacks. They have no beef with us. There beef is with the White man". This made me wonder who is responsible for these terrorist attacks on the Urban communities throughout the tri-state area and across America.

In January 1988, I called a meeting with some of my boys and discussed an organization I wanted to start called, N. V. H. A. - Non-Violent Hustlers Association. This ridiculous idea made stick-up kids even more anxious to get at me. Word spread throughout the neighborhood about this organization, and people said I was crazy and had lost my mind.

At the same time these things were going on, I was also preparing for my first shot at the Golden Gloves. My first Golden Glove fight was in March 1988. Dedication to fighting was my New Year's resolution. I was looking for a way out of this crime life because I was just tired of all the foolishness. Even though I was using drugs, I still trained. I just did not fight high. I got high after the fight.

One day while Wise and I were in the stairway of my building smoking woolers, we had a long discussion about our operation and life. I was pouting and telling him how much I was tired of the drug game and the violence that came with it. At the end of the conversation, he told me, "Man, shut the fuck up! You only have one life to live."

I told him I was serious and was through with that kind of lifestyle. I was going to retire from robbing, selling and using drugs, and that I was going to pursue my boxing career.

We agreed to split up the last bit of money we had made together after the Golden Gloves tournament and go our separate ways. When I walked back into my apartment, I was fed up. I went into my room and sat on my bed. Then I dropped to my knees and started crying, asking the Lord to take me off drugs and to give me a better life. Then I went to bed and woke up the next day and decided to go to the Jehovah Witness Kingdom Hall with my mother to say a prayer.

Wise and I smoking woolers in my room

Black and I holding a brick

CHAPTER 7: THE GOLDEN GLOVES

I was a pretty talented young boxer with a lot of street fighting technique. I called my shadow boxing "scientific boxing" and I would imitate Hector Camacho and Ali Lee. They were my hero fighters at the time and I tailor made my boxing style from them.

The Golden Gloves started in February of 1988. My first fight was scheduled for March 1988 at a school in the Bronx. My first opponent was a short, stocky Puerto Rican guy who's name I cannot recall. It was, at that time, the battle of my life, because this guy was very tough. He was a short, stocky guy who was hard to hit. He ducked a lot of my punches, but my jab connected frequently. By the second round, I was already tired. This guy was throwing right hands and hooks at my jaw but I was able to move my head and elude most of his punches.

My mother, Aunt Ruthy, Darryl and cousin Damian, looked on in horror. The contender was surging forward with a lot of pressure and swinging very hard punches. In the end, I came out the victorious winner and I have to say I had never been as tired in my entire life as I was after that fight. A day or two prior to the fight, I had smoked weed and crack, and drank, because I was still addicted and fighting my demons. The fight was a three rounder and even though it was very competitive, I won by decision.

After the fight, I went straight into the locker room and sprawled out on the floor in sheer exhaustion. I then jumped in the shower, which was a bad move, because I caught a serious cold afterward, from being really hot and sweaty to being cold, which wasn't a smart thing to do. I believe if I'd had a smarter trainer, he would've known that wasn't the right thing to do, especially with my next fight only a week away.

The next fight was at The Fort Apache boxing club in the Bronx. This fight was with an easy white boy by the name of Danny Danny. He was an unattached fighter. Basically, he dreamed of becoming a boxer, but hadn't trained for the fight. Usually guys who do not have much experience but still enter a competitive tournament like the Golden Gloves are just groupies and wannabes. I demolished him about twenty seconds into the first round. I hit him with a double jab, then a right hand, followed by a hook. I hit him with an uppercut, then back to the left, which had this guy spinning around like a spinning top with blood splattering all over the ring.

My next fight in the tournament was in the quarterfinals against another white boy that I assumed was soft like Danny Danny, but was I in for a rude awakening. He was this tall, lanky dude that looked like Five-O. His name was Michael Hospadore. In the first round, he began throwing hard hooks at me that made me think, "Goddamn, what the hell does he have in his gloves?" But with my good defense, I was able to get away from his fierce attack. However, like usual, I started getting tired by the second round, which made him press even harder to finish me off. I got tired so early because I was not in proper condition. I was smoking crack and smoking weed after every fight. I don't know what kind of spirit came over me but I refused to let this guy knock me out, let alone hit me. He missed about twenty hard left and right hooks. When the fight was over, I was so tired I could barely stand up. All of that slipping and moving to get out of his way used up a lot of energy. The referee had to raise my hands for me, while I was stumbling around the ring like those WWF wrestlers. The referee had the audacity to argue with me about being musty that night.

Right in the middle of the ring, while I was exhausted, he said in my ear, "You're a young man, you shouldn't be smelling like that." It is possible that drugs were sweating out of my body causing an unusual smell. Plus, I used to wear cheap deodorant so I guess I could have been musty. I just pulled my arm away from him and said, "Get the fuck off me, man." I was too tired to hear that bullshit. Anyway, musty or not, I beat Hospadore by decision.

My trainer, Johnny, had to help me walk out of the ring, and we had to walk up some steps to get to the dressing room. We didn't make it to the dressing room for another twenty minutes because I collapsed right on the steps. I think I had a mild heart attack which I suspect was caused by all of the weed and crack smoking I was doing. No doctor ever examined me at this time but I believe that it was a mild heart attack because it took me about half an hour to catch my breath.

Michael's trainer was staring down at me, wondering how in the hell did I beat his fighter with such bad conditioning. He just couldn't believe it. Bruce Silverglade, the owner of Gleason's Gym, walked to the exit where I was lying on the steps in sheer exhaustion. Enthusiastically, he came over and said, "Great fight, Mitch."

I just looked at him and nodded my head, as if to say thank you.

Michael's dream of becoming a Golden Glove champ that year was shattered, but the next year, he took the Golden Glove easily. He eventually turned pro but retired with a 3-0 record. I saw his last fight at a Manhattan arena, the same arena that I made my pro debut against Eddie Cruz. Michael fought a friend of mine named Jimmy Walker. I provided Jimmy with the tape of our fight so that he could study his technique. Michael won but he was really bruised and battered with a lot of blood trickling down his face. I saw him after the fight and we shook hands but he gave me an embarrassed look like he was fed up with boxing. I saw him at a local show a year later and he told me that that was his last fight and that now he is Nassau County Police officer.

A week later after my last fight, the semi-finals were next. They matched me up against this big, scary looking fighter named Michael Outerbridge. He had knocked out all three of his opponents thus far. I was intimidated by him but I was determined to fight him like a man. I thought he was going to annihilate me, but I fought under pressure and busted this guy up pretty bad. I counter punched him almost perfectly all the way through the fight, wobbling him a few times. He didn't want to fall, but he looked very embarrassed after that fight. I won by decision.

I had reached the Golden Gloves championship while on crack. I was 3-0 as an amateur boxer. Nobody thought it was possible that a guy like me from the projects would be competing in the finals. Mostly all the people I grew up around always spoke negatively about things I said I could achieve. I was only one of a few kids in the neighborhood who had a goal of becoming somebody.

People in the urban community can be like a barrel of crabs, wanting to pull you down because they're not going anywhere and did not have ambition to achieve a dream. That's a major problem with black youths in our community. We don't have goals or dreams. I think I was fortunate from being in Great Valley, because it gave me hope and made me want to become somebody and do something with my life. While it is true that I still had that criminal element inside of me, I was still young and at the same time I had a goal and a dream of trying to better myself. With just the little dreams that I was trying to accomplish, I felt unique because a lot of brothers in the hood did not have any goals at all.

Although we had a lot of negative people in the neighborhood, we did have positive people as well. I had a good amount of fans coming up. It was mainly the older people forty years and older who understood what I was trying to do. I have to admit, a lot of my fans were white and a lot of them were very encouraging and used to tell me to go for it. However, the majority of my fans were black.

Riddick Bowe, Kevin Kelly, Junior Jones, Michael Bent, all those guys were in the championship in 1988. I was a part of that team, and very proud to be. They all went on to become champions; unfortunately for me, I didn't.

In the finals I was up against this guy named Nathan Williams. We were the last two men standing in the heavyweight division. The association called our match "Brooklyn vs. The Bronx". Nate and I were the top two fighters standing at the end of the 1988 Golden Gloves. We were the best two amateurs in New York City at the time. I was so confident I had this tournament in the bag, I began drinking, smoking and having sex a couple days before the fight. I really didn't have a solid boxing team behind me so my partying and celebrating went unchecked. The Golden Glove competitors share the same dressing rooms while waiting for their bouts. While in the locker room waiting for my match with Nathan, I was using intimidating tactics to make him nervous by staring him down and giving him mean facial gestures. Then I started whistling showing him that I had no fear of him and that I thought he was a punk.

Nathan won the fight on a 3-2 decision. The guy was good and had great skills. He really surprised me. I had heard later on after the fight that he'd had about a hundred amateur fights before me. I'd only had three fights before him, which were those Golden Glove fights.

After the fight that night, Nathan admitted to me that he thought I'd won the fight. I won the first two rounds, and then ran out of gas. In the last round, I ran and counter punched him. I tried to get on that Hector Camacho shit - hit and run and hustle away. The judges didn't buy it, and gave the gold to him. I went into shock and was in a daze. As I walked away, I had flashbacks about the other fights I'd had in that tournament that I fought so hard to win. All those competitive bouts and hard work went right down the drain. My dream of becoming the Golden Glove champ was ruined.

When they gave me the silver gloves in the locker room, I put them on happily while everybody else that had gotten silver wasn't happy about wearing them. Riddick Bowe came in the locker room while I had my head down feeling depressed and said he thought I had won the golden gloves and that I would be able to stop popping shit now that I won. What he meant was that I did not have to keep bragging and telling everybody in the gym about what I am going to prove to them and the whole world about how wrong they are!! Since I was the type of guy that wasn't trying to hear people say "you can't do this, you can't do that," I just brushed his comments and feedback off, and continued to try and do what I dreamed I could do. Bowe trained with me in Bed Stuy while growing up. A week later, after the Golden Glove finals, it was revealed that Nathan Williams had lied about his age on the application and said he was 17 when he was really 16 years old. The amateur boxing federation told Nathan Williams to turn over the Golden Gloves to me but he never did and everybody's lips were sealed. This information was told to me by the famous cut man, Al Gavin while working out in Gleason's gym one day. Al Gavin was Lenox Lewis's cutman as well as a dozen other champions. Unfortunately, he died recently, may his soul rest in peace.

However, being in the finals of the Golden Gloves got me a lot of respect from my peers and foes. I quit dealing with a lot of people, and at the same time, a lot of people started to take me more seriously. I was the neighborhood hero and a big bad wolf in Brooklyn. From my picture being in the paper, I got much love from people.

When I ran into people that I hadn't seen in years, they told me they'd seen my championship fight in Madison Square Garden on MSG cable TV. Although I didn't get the gold, it made me very confident and even conceited.

I went back into the gym, firing bombs on my sparring partners. I was dancing around like Ali. Being in the finals made me believe even more that one day I could make it. Unfortunately, after the Golden Gloves, there was no support for the runner up, only for the champs. They got to go on trips around the world competing in other shows and getting more experience, while the runner-ups were abandoned to the streets. I had to wait a year for another amateur fight, for the next Golden Gloves.

For the next six months, my focus was on getting off crack and weed. I wanted to become a better conditioned fighter and focus more on my training. I had the same trainer, doing the same routine, which inhibited me from progressing mentally, as well as physically. So by the time the 1989 Golden Gloves tournament came around, I was doing just about the same things.

I did get off crack by going down south for about a week. I stayed in the woods in Alabama with some family and friends and drank corn liquor, home made liquor that they drank down South. This helped sweat the crack out of my system. Being drunk off it, gave me cravings for crack but I knew that I did not have access to it. Soon, the desire wore out of my body to the point that I did not want it anymore. The urge was minimized and eventually it was gone. That week gave me a head start to come home clean, because that was the longest amount of time I'd been off crack in about two years. After that trip, I never smoked crack again, plus I stopped selling it which meant since it wasn't in my presence at the time, I was not tempted to smoke again.

However, I continued to smoke weed and drink. I still had that ghetto mentality that as long as I wasn't using hard stuff like crack or heroin, weed and liquor weren't too bad.

Me after scientific shadow boxing

Victory over Outerbridge at Golden Gloves

With trainer JohnnyBoy, after Golden Gloves

After semi finals with trainer JohnnyBoy, Mom, Aunt and Mateen

CHAPTER 8: GOLDEN GLOVES, ROUND TWO

When the 1989 Golden Gloves arrived, I had anticipated getting the gold that year. My first fight was up against a police officer from Long Island, another Michael. He heard about me from last year, so he was very nervous from the start. I hit him with one body shot. He hollered ouch and backed up to surrender so the ref would stop the fight. The punch wasn't even that hard. He just gave up, more from intimidation than anything else. He made me feel like I was George Foreman.

The semi finals were next. Once again I was up against Michael Outerbridge, the guy I had demolished last year. In our rematch, he was still upset with me from last year for shattering his dreams and he wanted payback. I was still a conceited fighter, and knew I could beat this guy.

I beat Outerbridge up the first two rounds, bruised and dazed him really good. I had him spiraling out of control, spinning around the ring, but he caught his composure and continued to fight. He did the same thing Nathan Williams did in our fight last year in the Golden Gloves. He picked up the pace and hustled in the last round. He was swinging wild, with a lot of anger, but he was missing the same way Nathan had missed. I was playing with this guy, taunting and smacking him around the ring like a bitch, while he was swinging like a girl.

One of my corner men, Bob Jackson, was screaming at me, saying, "Outerbridge is killing you!"

I screamed back at Bob, "No way, he ain't doin' nothin'!"

Bob had experience on how they judged

amateur fights. I didn't know that even if you beat this guy in the first two rounds he could win fights just by throwing air punches or hitting a guy on the arms and rallying in the last round. This shit was all new to me. I was pissed off.

When the crowd saw me yelling at my corner man, they booed me. I waved my hand back at them and said, "Shut the fuck up!" They booed even louder. If anything, the judges took the fight from me because of bad sportsmanship. Deep down inside, I knew I hadn't lost the fight. Outerbridge also knew I had won the fight, even though they gave it to him.

After that fight, I felt like there was a conspiracy against me because I had lost the Golden Gloves two years straight. That year I didn't get any meaningful fights either. I entered the Spanish Gloves a tournament in the Bronx, and won by a walkover, which meant there was nobody to fight. There was one other guy in the tournament, but when he and his people saw that it was me he had to fight, they backed out. I was a feared competitor in the amateurs. During the next year while waiting for another opportunity at the Golden Gloves, I was pretty much inactive, except for a minimal amount of training in the gym. Again my trainer, Johnny, wasn't teaching me anything new, just the same old routine. He had me jabbing the bag and doing a few rounds with my sparring partner once or twice a week. He didn't have me doing any pad work or hitting the speed bag and hardly any sit ups or jump rope. Even though I had terrible training and teaching, my scientific shadow boxing was sufficient enough to help me to not get seriously hurt.

I entered the Golden Gloves in 1990, once again with hardly any conditioning and training. I felt that I was a talented enough boxer to beat these guys with literally no training. That year I drank all the way up to the night of the fight. This time things were starting to get out of hand as I got older and more ridiculous. I drank two or three 40 ounces of Olde English the night before the fight.

My first fight in the 1990 Golden Gloves was at the Elks Club in Queens, New York. I was a super heavyweight by then, weighing 210 pounds. My opponent a fellow by the name of Bear weighed 320 pounds. We battled the whole three rounds, and Bear wasn't able to touch me. Even though I was out of shape, I took him to school and he knew it. He thought I had won the fight. The crowd even knew I'd won, and that I had put on a good show. The judges, though, said he had won. I just couldn't understand why they kept taking the fights from me.

After this fight my bad conditioning really showed. When the fight was over, and while they were announcing the decision, I collapsed right in the middle of the ring from sheer exhaustion. I had had too much to drink the night before and I'd lost total control of my equilibrium. While lying on the canvas, one of the EMT workers gave me oxygen, which made me feel even more like I couldn't breath. I pushed the mask off my face and declined the oxygen.

The EMT said, "What are you doing? It's only air". I just shook my head no, because all I really needed was a little bit of rest to wind down. I was stretched out for about fifteen minutes like I'd been knocked unconscious. When I finally regained enough strength, I was helped to my feet and was able to walk on my own. The crowd gave me a standing ovation, showing they cared and was concerned about me. That feeling was better than winning the fight, and the best thing about it was the majority of the crowd was white. I was delighted to know people of another race showed that kind of concern for me. Since most of the crowd was white, I assumed that they came to see two guys beat the shit out of each other not show concern when somebody drops dead. My friend, Dennis, was with me at the fight, along with my girlfriend, Delores, who looked very concerned for me.

That night my trainer, Johnny Boy, told me that if I was going to continue to drink and do drugs before fights, I might as well not fight anymore. He asked me "What was the sense of fighting if I never got into shape"? That was true, but I felt like he should've pushed me more in training and taught me how to exercise, but apparently he didn't know how. We never talked about this training issue because at the time, I still did not understand the proper way to train.

However, he did warn me that if I decided to turn pro, not to let the promoters and matchmakers use me. He also stressed that in order to turn pro, I'd have to be in serious shape, and that he wasn't going out there with me in my state of mind and conditioning.

He talked about how I could get myself killed or seriously hurt, but I was young and didn't want to hear that. I believed I could beat a pro fighter even if I wasn't really in good shape. I thought I was just that talented.

1990 Golden Glove fight with 320 lb opponent Bear, passed out after fight

CHAPTER 9: AMATEUR NO MORE: GOING PRO

In 1991, I stood at five, eleven and a half and weighed 250 pounds. I had only been in the gym about fifteen days out of a month, but I was still looking for a fight. I didn't have a manager nor a promoter, but I had the audacity to think I was going somewhere in boxing. I was a stubborn boxer with no direction in life. I had no job, no money, and I didn't know how to hustle anymore. It had been a while since I was hustling and the drug game had changed. Now, a lot of young, up and coming kids had taken over and these guys were more violent than I was. I hadn't even attended college or a trade school for backup just in case boxing didn't work out. My counselor Terry at Great Valley used to tell me that I had a ninety-five percent chance of not making it in sports. But I was hardheaded and didn't listen to him.

I was working out at Gleason Gym in Brooklyn, and Bruce Silverglade, the owner of the gym, asked me if I wanted to fight on a show coming up. The matchmaker for the show was Joel Judah, the father of former lightweight champion, Zab Judah.

Joel had asked me also to fight on the show, even though he knew I wasn't in shape to fight. At the time, he was supposed to be my friend, but he didn't care about what could've happened to me. He just wanted to fill up the card for the promoter, Ron Stevens, who eventually became New York's Boxing Commissioner. When Ron offered to pay me a measly four hundred dollars for the fight, he just looked at me like I was a hungry wolf. I didn't care; I took it because I was tired of being broke.

Plus, Delores and I had moved into an apartment together, and I needed the rent money. The rent was six hundred dollars a month and I had to pay half. The building we moved into was called Linden Plaza Projects. It was a whole lot nicer than LaFayette Gardens Projects. The people said good morning and good night to each other, and that was a miracle for living in a project in Brooklyn, especially East New York.

Johnny Boy refused to train me for the fight, because he said I wasn't in shape and that they were just using me. We got into a heated argument about me taking that fight. I told him he wasn't a good trainer anyway, and that I was quitting and doing what I wanted to do. He told me to go for it, but that I'd see what those people out there in the boxing world would do to me.

* * *

The night I fought Eddie Cruz there was a relatively small crowd, about two or three hundred people, at the Marriott Hotel in Manhattan on 34th Street. My old neighbors, Emanuel Lewis and his mother were there. Emanuel was the only one from our projects that made it out and became famous. He played Webster on a television sitcom. He and his mother were cheering me on.

The fight was over in two rounds and I was glad because I started feeling fatigue come on very early. Eddie and I collided heads, and I felt his razor thin hair up against my head when it cut me. The legendary Emile Griffith had helped work my corner that night, and he was the one that looked at my cut and decided to stop the fight. The middle of my head was cut from a head butt. I needed about six stitches to close it. Eddie had been winning, but I had also been taking him to school before I started feeling fatigue. I really couldn't tell what the outcome would have been, because I was an unpredictable fighter and had been able to fight back while I was tired in the past. That was all I knew how to be tired in a fight and continue on because I had never been in shape for a fight before.

After the fight, Eddie yelled at me, "I was gonna knock you out, punk!" Bleeding from the head, I just looked at him because there was really nothing I could say. After I paid everyone for helping me, I walked away with two hundred and sixty dollars. I gave Eddie Post forty dollars as a training fee, which was ten percent. I gave Emile Griffith one hundred dollars for helping with my cut and being there for me. But I still did not have all of my rent money.

I felt like people inside the arena were looking at me saying, "You were a goddamn fool".

The next morning after the fight, I woke up sad and depressed. I felt like I had no direction in my life. I had already departed from Wise and the drug game over a year or two ago, so I was wondering how the hell I was gonna make it. I felt safe knowing I had moved out of LaFayette Gardens, cause I didn't have to worry about all kinds of thugs looking for me, or getting into a beef with somebody.

In LaFayette Gardens, dudes came out of the building with mean faces, they didn't smile, and if you smiled at them, they wanted to know what was funny. Growing up in the projects, a lot of us didn't have anything to smile about. Our mothers were either on crack or alcohol, in jail or sick from some sort of disease. A lot of the brothers were criminals without money or a future to look forward to. That's why in Linden Plaza, I pretty much tried to stay to myself and do me. I did not want any friends because friends in the hood always talk behind your back, stole from you and tried to pull you down to their level. They would even try to eventually harm or possibly kill you. Especially, because the majority of those dudes in the projects grew up with no morals and principles.

At Gleason's Gym

CHAPTER 10: SPARRING PARTNER

I had only fought eight times as an amateur, which made me pretty inexperienced as a professional boxer. Not too many people in the boxing business were willing to take a chance with investing in a fighter like that, because the odds were against you. Nobody was in the business to lose money, let alone have a boxer that was losing fights.

Fortunately, for me, I had a lot of natural talent and a great amount of street fights, plus I had created a lot of techniques at home. I created good defensive skills and foot movements. The skills I developed at home enabled me to elude a great percentage of punishment in my boxing career, whether it was in sparring or in a real fight.

However, boxing managers were real keen and good hustlers. The managers and promoters were friends and worked together when formulating boxing shows. Most of the promoters were Jews and the managers were mostly Italians. Managers usually picked out an investment fighter by his background. How many fights he had, how many he'd lost, what amateur titles he'd won, and what condition he was in were part of the decision. A fighter's conditioning was his stock. Without it, he wouldn't go far.

Unfortunately, I learned that late in my career. Most of the time, a manager would try to avoid matching his fighter up against a well conditioned fighter. His goal was to catch a fighter off guard; to get guys that weren't really in condition but hungry for some money. He'd look for a struggling boxer with no job, not knowing where his next fight or meal was coming from. I used to call that the devil's code.

The club fighter would only get six days to prepare, while the star would get six weeks and six months of tuning up to prepare. The difference between tuning up and training is that a boxer who is tuning up has had other fights to remain sharp. A boxer who is tuning up gets consistent fights from promoters. A club fighter who is just training is in the gym and has not had any recent fights in any public arena. This was how the managers made their living. It was a racket and apparently a good hustle because a lot of guys got rich from those schemes. And that's why managers usually get rid of a fighter if he loses one or two fights. (Remember, the promoters and managers are not your friends. You are their investment only.) However, I believe it's unfair and a fighter should have the opportunity to lose at least five times before they decide to kick you out of their stable. I wanted to beat the odds by knocking out one of those up and coming heavyweight prospects. That's why I tried to manage and promote myself. I just didn't do it with the right conditioning and the proper six to eight weeks preparation time.

When you're young and naïve, you don't have the slightest idea what goes on in boxing. You're thinking it's a fair sport, but it's not. Even if you win a fight clean, the judges will sometimes steal the fight from you, because they're working for the promoters of the show, and they have to favor his fighter or they won't get any more work from them. The judges are very intimidated by the promoters, and the managers pay the promoters to put their fighters on the cards. The promoters pressure their matchmakers to make sure they find an opponent who's not in shape and doesn't have enough training time to be ready.

So, if you're not down with a connected manager who's going to lay down some money for you to get easy wins, you're pretty much doomed. Even if you're a knockout artist, they'll just avoid you and watch you grow gray hair. Basically, boxing is another hustle. Promoters also pay for their fighters to be ranked the majority of the time. If you pay some money, you can go from being Top 20 to #2 or #3 in the ranking.

It took me years to realize that, but when I finally did, I said to myself, "Damn, I would've preferred baseball or basketball." I'm trying to get away from negativity and corruption, but I always seem to land right back in it anyway. Bottom line, boxing is the most corrupt and unregulated professional sport.

Boxing is ruled by a group of people that never even put on a pair of gloves before. The commentators got their jobs because it was passed down from one generation to another. The boxing industry is one big circus. Half of the commissioners were taxi drivers before they became commissioner or wannabee local promoters who only promoted approximately two boxing shows. No other experience is required. And the scoring of boxing is terrible. The Compu box scoring, in my opinion, is as rigged as political voting ballets.

Boxing fans and the audience criticize boxers for blowing these so called millions of dollars they make. Fans are not aware that the managers and promoters are stealing from the fighters. For example, a promoter brokers a deal for his fighter with HBO for three million dollars. He lies to his fighter and tells him it was one million he brokered. .

Therefore the promoter pockets two million then he takes 30 percent of a fighter's one million dollar purse which gives him a grand total of 2.3 million. Then the manager gets 15 percent of the fighter's purse. Then the trainer gets 10 percent and then three percent to the "cut man". Plus miscellaneous fees and 25 percent in taxes so when you round off the fighter's purse, he winds up with around $300,000 out of three million. When I fought Butterbean, it was alleged that Bruce made $8,500 for a matchmaking fee but told me the fight was only for $1,500. This is how they have been cheating boxers since boxing started. If they do not start regulating boxing more legitimately, I think what fighters ought to start doing is making examples out of promoters and managers by ski-masking and tying them up then turning them upside down and shaking them like a piggy bank.

Plus we have terrible trainers out there. Most of the trainers are bootleg and so phony that all they do is brag about the fights that they never had. As soon as you tap them with a midsection body shot they curl up like a snail. They are so stupid that after the fighter has a ten round bout and took about a hundred punches, trainers still aggressively rub fighters' heads talking about, "Great fight! Great fight!" not even acknowledging how much punishment their fighter's brain suffered. And the trainers who actually fought and attained some kind of glory are so egotistical that they think that most of the fighters do not have what it takes and can not possibly be as good as them. They walk around still believing that they are champions appearing on every local boxing show just for publicity and the opportunity to be seen. There aren't too many good trainers in boxing anymore. All the good trainers gave up because every time they built up a fighter the boxer eventually got stolen by a slick, rich, white businessman that bribed the fighter by offering him money to leave his trainer, that sacrificed years of hard work and dedication developing his boxing techniques. A good example is the late trainer George Washington, who trained former heavy-weight champion Riddick Bowe and former welter-weight champion Mark Breland. Mr. Washington prepared both of these guys for the Olympic gold medal. After they won, they abandoned him and went with other people that had influence and money in the boxing industry. Mark Breland let George carry his spit bucket for a while in some of his fights. But eventually abandoned him totally, leaving him broke with a bruised ego and failing health in the Bed-Stuy Boxing Association Gym in Brooklyn.

The referees are the only ones in boxing who really have boxing experience but they are paid the least. Yet the judges never fought a day in their life and they make a ton of money. Many of them have just recently been arena security guards and then out of the blue one day you will see them working as a boxing judge! What I do know is that the boxing industry has close ties with each other. They are so close that half of the industry is controlled by homosexuals. I witnessed with my own eyes a very prestigious boxing official walking in Brooklyn Heights, with another man suspiciously. They entered the restaurant and had an intimate dinner.

Regardless, boxing has always been a goal for me. It's hard for me to say I regret becoming a boxer, because without it, I don't know where I'd get my strength from. While all my friends fell victim to the street poisons, I remained standing and fighting. I fought drugs, alcohol, sex, crime, and continued to strive to be the best I could be. To me, that's worth more than being a millionaire and being famous. I got my pride and dignity from boxing. But with all that pride and dignity, I still had to find a way to make a living. That's why I constantly went back to Gleason's Gym to continue trying to get in shape somehow, some way. I was still training myself most of the time, and would try to hustle in the gym by helping white collar guys train for the white collar boxing shows Bruce Silverglade was throwing.

Those shows consisted of mostly businessmen competing in exhibition fights. Bruce also knew I was broke and a struggling boxer so he used to constantly offer me jobs to be the sparring partner for various fighters. One of my first encounters was with a guy named Jeremy Williams. He was being trained by Kevin Ronney, Mike Tyson's former trainer. Jeremy is currently one of the trainers on the TV show The Contenders. I jumped on the train and rode all the way to the Catskills to work with Jeremy.

We sparred for four days straight. I handled him pretty well for the first couple of days, but then my conditioning started to catch up to me. I started getting tired by the second round of sparring, and that's when Jeremy started going in for the kill. He wanted to knock me out because he was frustrated that he couldn't connect a clean punch the way he wanted to. After a couple of days, however, I felt abandoned being all the way in the Catskills without any family, staying in a hotel and eating cold cuts for breakfast. I told Kevin that I could not live this way anymore and that I was leaving. The time frame for staying to spar depended on how one performed and the fight schedule of your sparring partner. My condition was not that good to continue to compete with Jeremy. Plus, I just had enough of the camp out type of lifestyle. Kevin paid me five hundred dollars, and I jumped on the train back to New York.

A month later, I went to New Jersey to give Shannon Briggs some sparring. Bruce thought that maybe I would be in better shape by now and figured I needed to make money. He didn't care about what happened to me in camp. Trainers called the gym looking for sparring partners and he just delivered and tried to give good customer service. I was still out of shape and Mr. Briggs tried to kill me. We battled for three rounds. He got so frustrated with my defense that he hit me with an illegal blow to the back of my head that hurt and dazed me. Then he tried to go in for the kill and knock me out, but I was able to escape. Teddy Atlas, Brigg's trainer had the audacity to ask me to go one more round after being punched in the back of my head. I told him no and that I was finished because the guy was fighting dirty. He paid me a hundred dollars for one day's work. I left the camp and headed back to the city with another failed attempt at beating up one of those nurtured and up and coming heavyweight contenders.

* * *

A couple months later, Bruce Silverglade asked me if I wanted to go to the Catskills again to spar with Bruce Seldon, who was preparing for a big fight with Tony Tubs.

I had my own car by then, an old Chevy I bought at an auction for $150. I drove two and a half hours to the mountains. I was a competitor like those Chinese guys in those karate flicks, who challenged fighters all over the world to find out how good they were. As usual, I went unprepared and out of shape, which was my MO.

After boxing Bruce Seldom for three days, he fractured my nose with that jackhammer jab he possessed. I was so disappointed I couldn't give Bruce quality work I packed up and told him I was leaving camp. Bruce asked me if I was gonna wait for his manager to come so I could get paid, I told him I didn't deserve to get paid because of the way I came all the way up there and performed. I jumped in my beat up car with a fractured nose and headed back to Brooklyn. Eventually Bruce got a shot at Mike Tyson for five million dollars. The match only lasted for one round. I ran into Bruce on Fulton Street in downtown Brooklyn six months after the Tyson fight and asked him if I could get my fee for helping him prepare for Tony Tubbs. Bruce responded by telling me that I had to ask his manager for that money and that he was not responsible which kind of pissed me off. So I told him that I had a Rolex for sale. He fell for it and paid me $800 dollars for a two-tone Oyster Bay counterfeit Rolex, otherwise known as a Bolex.

In 1992, I was still hanging around the gym, broke and trying to figure out where next month's rent money was coming from. I decided to ask Bruce Silverglade for another fight. He offered me a fight against this white guy with a 4-1 record, by the name of Tim Agle. I didn't do my homework on the dude, didn't watch any tapes of his fights, didn't know his amateur background, and to be honest, I didn't care because I needed the money to pay my rent. Plus, I just wanted to be able to fight someone inside of an arena.

At the time of the fight, I was weighing an embarrassing 250 pounds. A supposed friend of mine, a boxer by the name of Ernest, knew the guy I was fighting the whole time but stayed quiet until I was in

Binghamton, New York at the arena. Then all of sudden he said, "Hey, I know that guy. He won the Olympic trials. He's a real tough guy." That's how Ernest was, always a snake.

Even if he would have told me that back home, knowing me, I would not have listened anyway because I was still hardheaded, and did not have much respect for any fighter anyway.

The fight was televised out in Binghamton because Tim Agle was a local star boxer there. I figured that was why all the people were screaming and hollering for him. When I came out, people were booing really loud. They booed even louder when their star couldn't knock me out.

When the fight began, that's when I realized how out of shape I was. I could hardly throw a decent punch, let alone knock somebody out. I knew right then I was in for a long night. He was throwing punches at me like a robot; he just kept coming at me. He was a great fighter who was in superb shape. I couldn't do anything to him. I knew that if I kept punching at him he was going to counter me and possibly hurt or knock me out.

When the fight was over, they booed me out of the arena, but I was too busy trying to catch my breath and stand on my own two feet to really care. Even though I had lost the fight, Tim turned out to be a bigger loser because later the town was laughing and criticizing him about not knocking out an out of shape guy like me. After that, Tim broke up with his management team and retired from fighting.

Local boxing critics said the reason he retired was because he was embarrassed and ashamed for not putting on a good show for his hometown crowd. So, if I was a loser, then what would you call him?

Even though he used me for what they wanted which was an opponent to get a win from, the promoter was so mad at me that he didn't want to pay for a room for me to stay until the next day. Someone told me the promoter said I had to use my own money to pay for a room, which was four hundred dollars. I had that same clown trainer, Eddie Post, with me, being that Johnny Boy and I had parted ways. Eddie was the same guy that was in my corner for the Eddie Cruz fight. I also had a neighborhood friend with me named Cheese. He was a former boxer that helped work my corner. The guys that were up there with me felt so bad, they didn't even want a cut of the money I had earned.

I was saved by this white guy named Robert who was a sports writer. I had seen him around Golden Gloves boxing shows before. He saw me fight in Madison Square Garden as an amateur. Now, he was writing for a magazine called Boxing Digest. He even wrote a few articles about me later on in my career. This guy had believed in me since my amateur days, and was someone I will always call a friend. He was also a sincere boxing advocate. He offered me space in his room. He went out, got a cot and told me I could have the bed and that he'd sleep on the cot. The next day, I went back to Brooklyn with nowhere to go and a 0-2 record.

CHAPTER 11: JEWELRY HEIST

I was pretty much a lost fighter with no direction in my life. All I had was my girlfriend, Delores, and an apartment even if I didn't know where my rent money was coming from. I was so broke that I started pawning the little bit of jewelry I had left. It got to the point that I became addicted to pawning my jewelry. I even started asking Delores to pawn her jewelry too.

One day, I was in the Gem pawnshop in downtown Brooklyn waiting in line to pawn some jewelry, and I had such a sad look on my face, that it seemed as though the security guard could feel my predicament and hardship. He started staring at me, saying he hated those crackers. That they were full of shit in this store, and that he wanted to get them robbed. I just stood there listening to him as he spoke. Eventually, he crept up on me. The guy went as far as following me out the store, asking me whether I knew someone who'd be willing to rob those crackers.

When I got back to the projects, I told some of the local guys about my encounter with the security guard. Word spread around the projects, and a couple of stick-up kids heard about the opportunity. Next thing you know, word had spread around the neighborhood that somebody in the projects had pulled off the jewelry heist. Some people assumed it was me because I had knowledge of the situation beforehand.

I was getting strange looks and some people were joking with me saying, "Come on man, we know you had something to do with that jewelry heist. "The rumors had gotten so bad to the point that I started joking that I was as innocent as William Shatner, who allegedly killed his wife.

I went to Gleason's Gym to get a workout and while in the locker room, I was talking to my sparring partner Ernest. I joked with him about some boys I knew that had stuck up a jewelry store, and how they had given me some of the gold they heisted. I told him the store's name, which coincidently, happened to be the pawn shop that Ernest had his jewelry and Golden Gloves in. After telling him about the heist, Ernest saw dollar signs and a possible opportunity to profit from it. I joked about the store because I always liked to brag and boast about the things that happened in the hood.

He asked me, "Yo, can I get a hundred dollars?"

I responded, "No, I don't have a hundred dollars."

Ernest went home, called the pawnshop and brokered a deal with the owner. The deal was he would turn in the people responsible for the robbery, and in return, he'd get his Golden Gloves and jewelry out for free. Ernest met with the police and told them I had gone to his house with a bag full of gold and tried to sell it to him, but he didn't have the money. The police and Ernest took a ride around the projects so that he could point us out. He rode around in a van with tinted windows, and pointed out the car I was driving. He also pointed out my boys, Dembo and Cee.

The detectives followed me for about two months, hoping to catch me wearing some of the jewelry. They were also watching Dembo and Cee. Eventually they decided to arrest and charge us with the crime. I was the first one they arrested. They followed me from East New York to Bedstuy. When I went to the park, the detectives came from behind, pulled me over and cuffed me. The police had already been gathering evidence against me. They already had the security guard and his friend apprehended. They also had statements from Ernest as a witness.

While in the precinct, they interrogated me, and were able to get some pretty incriminating statements out of me. They showed me a picture of the security guard and said that he told them I was involved in the robbery. Like a fool, I didn't take full advantage of my rights by not saying anything. I was too busy arguing with them about my innocence. I told them the security guard had asked me to do it, but that I had refused. The police didn't have much evidence, but with those statements and Ernest's allegations, the court system believed I was involved.

While I was locked up, I called the pay phone around the neighborhood and spoke with a friend of mine named Junes, better known on the streets as Bar-Kim. That's what everyone from around the way did when they got locked up. They called that same pay phone on the corner and struck up a conversation with a passerby. People in the neighborhood used pay phones on a regular basis. That's how it was in the hood. The corner phone was it. Drug dealers did their business on the pay phones. Whores conducted their business on the pay phone. And every other hustler did business on those pay phones. They used to have call back numbers but the NYPD cracked down on them because they were used for a lot of criminal transactions and they were untraceable.

Those guys were aware that the detectives were looking for them, but they didn't understand why, so they didn't go into hiding. The detectives raided them in the lobby of the building where we lived the next day. There are really no true friends in the hood. Everybody is crossing each other and talking behind each other's back. There is not much loyalty and people in the hood like to spread rumors and lies about someone just to sensationalize a story. Cee and Dembo felt that they had no reason to hide about a jewelry store robbery. They knew that they had done robberies before just not at a jewelry store. And they knew that I was not the straightest guy in the neighborhood but this rumor was unacceptable.

When I went to my arraignment, I was offered one year but turned it down. Even though I didn't have a real criminal record, they still gave me a high bail of fifteen thousand dollars. I had a juvenile record, which is supposed to be sealed when you reach sixteen years old, however, authorities still peek at the record and judge you by your past deeds. They gave Dembo and Cee the same amount of bail as mine. When I spoke with my court appointed attorney, I asked him if he could get me a lower bail. He asked me what I could afford and I told him five thousand dollars. I knew my mother had about five thousand put away because I used to see her bank statements laying around the house so I felt that was the most realistic amount to offer. He said he'd ask the judge for a bail reduction, and that I should be eligible because of my clean record. The only record I had was when I was a juvenile. As an adult, my record was clean. The judge agreed and reduced my bail.

The day I came home, after two weeks of incarceration, was the same night I impregnated Delores. If I hadn't gotten that bail reduction, my first baby girl probably wouldn't have been conceived. I credited my lawyer, David Epstein, for that, and to this day, we still remain friends. I usually visit his office. He now has his own private practice. He specializes in criminal, personal injury, malpractice and slip and falls.

As for Dembo and Cee, their bail remained the same, and since they weren't able to make bail, they had to stay in jail for sixteen months until the trial. Cee was housed in the Brooklyn House jail, and Dembo was housed on Rykers Island. They used to come to court looking like slaves; handcuffed, wearing baggy and dingy clothes and sad faces. They were in this situation because of the word of an ex-convict named Ernest, not a good Samaritan who fabricated a story for his own personal gain. Ernest made up a story just to have us convicted and sent to jail for a long time. He had hidden hate and jealousy which he harbored against me. He was a boxer who went to jail for two years during his career and it was like he had a vendetta to put other people in jail too, so he went undercover as a secret informer.

* * *

Ernest used to hang around me at the gym and in my apartment. I used to give him money, and he was supposed to be my homeboy. He and I used to be sparring partners. He had been boxing longer than I but he saw how quickly I started catching on to the sport. For the first couple of months, he used to rough me up in sparring sessions, but then I started getting his number and putting some heavy combinations on him. He eventually started shying away from sparring matches with me.

Back in 1988, we were both in the Golden Gloves together and I reached the championship with him. He felt I shouldn't have been there because it was my first year in the Golden Gloves and he'd already been there twice and lost. He also knew that I was a drug dealer who smoked weed and drank, who did not train hard and kept a pocket full of money. When I fought Outerbridge in the semi-finals, Ernest's father helped work my corner. I displayed some remarkable skills and his father was so impressed that he bragged about how good and smart I was as a fighter. For a while, he'd tease Ernest that I was a smarter fighter and Ernest never took that well. From then on, he displayed a lot of animosity toward me. He acted like we were cool but deep down inside, he despised what I stood for.

* * *

While going back and forth to court, I was trying to find a more honest way to make a living. When a case is pending against you, it takes time to make it to trial. The prosecutors and lawyers debate the case which is constantly getting postponed until all the evidence and witnesses are prepared to start trial or bargain a plea. I started going on job interviews. It appeared that every interview I went on, there was a young white guy doing the interviewing. I was about 23 years old and I didn't have any job experience but I did have a high school diploma. All they would tell me was that they would call me back and for me not to call them. These white dudes used to look like they were laughing at me on the inside. They made me feel like I was begging and pleading for a handout. In my opinion, they didn't like my style, the way I looked and my tone of voice.

I was so depressed from going on interviews that I went back to the gym to alleviate the tension. As I was working out, this strange Jewish lady that used to be in the gym in Bed Stuy with all of us, asked me why I was looking so sad. She was strange to me because here she was this little old Jewish lady who may have been in her 50s hanging around mostly black people in a sweaty gym in the middle of one of the most violent neighborhoods in New York City. And she did not seem to care or worry about anything. I told her that it was rough because nobody wanted to hire me. She told me I wasn't the type of guy who worked for people, that I was more of a self-employed type of person. I was looking at her like she was a psychic or something. Working for myself had crossed my mind a couple of times but I didn't know how to react. She made me believe I could do it. She was a self-employed artist who worked out in the gym and painted pictures on a sketch pad that she always had with her when she came to the gym. She brought the pad to the gym after spending time painting pictures of children playing in ghetto parks.

From that day forward, I took heed to what she had said and I came up with a plan. I scrambled up three hundred dollars by borrowing two hundred from Delores, and one hundred from my mother. I went to a car auction and bought a used car for a hundred and fifty dollars. The other car I had broke down. At the time, I couldn't afford insurance, so I bought a bogus policy. The hustlers were selling fake insurance cards that expired in a year. At a Sheriff's auction, you do not have to register a car, only the Department of Motor Vehicles does that. At the auction, you have to hire one of the tow trucks on the premises to take your car home or to a garage. Then you take the bogus insurance card with the title to the Department of Motor Vehicles and register the car. So the registration is real but the insurance card is counterfeit. Then I bought me a taxicab sign from a stationary store, and started driving an illegal taxicab. In New York, you can buy a taxi sign in almost every auto parts store or stationary store. So my taxicab sign was official. It was the same sign all the other taxicabs use on the streets. I knew that the most that could happen if I got caught was that I'd get a fine for not having insurance or a taxicabs permit.

Back then in 1992, they didn't lock people up for that, they didn't even lock people up for not having a driver's license or a suspended license. That's when New York traffic accidents were at an all time high. People were getting run over by cars all day long. You had dudes riding around with one hundred plus traffic tickets and suspensions on their driving record until Mayor Giuliani cleaned up that mess. Mayor Giuliani passed new laws that made it a felony to ride around with a suspended license. Giuliani was a former prosecutor who started getting tough on certain crimes and violations in the city. He did a lot of cleaning up with the quality of life crimes.

I drove a "dollar cab". A "dollar cab" is the same as a taxicab except when you drove a "dollar cab", you followed the bus route and picked up passengers as opposed to driving all over the city to find them. I'd drive to bus stops picking up waiting passengers. I eventually started picking people up anywhere in the streets. Being a taxi in New York wasn't a picnic that's for sure. I picked up all kinds of people, drug dealers, prostitutes, even murderers. I could not prove that anyone was a murderer but I would just listen to some of the stuff they would say. They talked about drug spots and beef with this guy or that guy. They were talking about criminal activity and any criminal is capable of murder. I used to have a lot of conversations with my passengers, and they would tell me all kinds of stories. I was offered drugs, sex, and all kinds of negative activities for a cab ride. Some of the passengers would laugh at me because they knew I wasn't a real taxi, while others tried to show concern because they knew how dangerous it was to drive a taxi in New York. A lot of people used to tell me to be careful because they knew I was just a young man trying to make a living. Some respected the fact that I wasn't out there robbing and stealing.

Once in a while, I would get pulled over by the police and get ticketed, but I never got caught by the Taxi and Limousine Commission. They were rarely around, or just not enforcing the law. I didn't make a lot of money but I was able to survive. I would bring home sixty to a hundred dollars a day. It was enough to pay my rent and help put food on the table to feed my lady and newborn baby.

Sometimes my cars would break down and leave me stranded. I had to struggle up a couple more hundred dollars to buy a new car. Those old cars that I used to buy might have lasted for about three to four months before they broke down. I was doing so bad that I had to ask Delores to let me pawn some of her old jewelry she had saved from previous relationships. I would pawn her jewelry then eventually get it out. Then when times got hard again, I would re-pawn the jewelry. It became a routine. I started depending on pawning gold every time I got into a jam. This is why I said it became addictive. Still, Delores felt the jewelry was of sentimental value. I felt that if she wasn't with the nigga anymore, why the fuck did she still want to hold onto the jewelry he bought her. She eventually gave the jewelry up. I pawned it and used the money to buy me a real taxi from the auction. It was not a legit cab. It was just a used taxi that was confiscated by the Sheriff's Department because the owner had tickets. It already had a partition installed, which made things a little bit safer. This was better than the regular four door cars I had been using as a taxi. However, none of the cars had legitimate paper work. Still, being a taxi driver was a very dangerous occupation.

One day I picked up two people who looked like crackheads on Lexington Avenue. It was a very dark block and they were hesitant to make a move. It was a lady and a man, and I recognized the man. He was the son of George Washington, the trainer who trained Riddick Bowe and Mark Breland. I think he realized that I was someone he'd seen before, and that's probably what made him change his mind about robbing and possibly killing me. All crackheads are not necessarily murderers and this guy had seen me in the gym before. Also, he was raised by a good father, Mr. Washington, so I felt he should have known better. I saw him a few times after that, but never confronted him, nor did I mention it to Mr. Washington. Mr. Washington had even trained me previously and he had worked my corner when I defeated Butterbean.

A few other incidents took place while I was driving the cab. Once this Jamaican guy had me on this dead end block and it appeared he had a gun and was getting ready to rob me but first he asked me if I was an American. I said yes and he said "Cool, you all right." He told me he didn't like Haitian taxi drivers because they tried to charge people too much money and that they had an attitude problem like they think they are better than other cultures of black people. I was just happy to be alive. He then told me to wait, that he'd be back with my money but he vanished into the darkness. He jumped out and never returned. I guess he changed his mind about robbing me.

This other guy I took to these projects named Ebbot Fields in Brooklyn said, "How much?" When we got to his destination, I told him five dollars and he jumped out my cab and yelled, "Come get it ma'fucka!"

I was so heated I wanted to kill him. The day before, I had my gun with me for protection, but that day I didn't have it with me. I just sat in my car looking at that young dude walking away with his pants sagging down, saying to myself, if only I had my gun, I would've popped him right in his ass.

I would rent my taxi out once in a while, but every day was becoming more intolerable. Brothers around the way that I'd grown up with were laughing at me, talking about how I was supposed to have been all that back in the day but now I was a total loser and an unsuccessful boxer. That was the mentality brothers had in the hood. I was making some money and always kept about fifty dollars in my pocket. They were always broke but still they laughed at me. I even picked up this girl I'd known back in high school when I was the man. She asked what happened to me. Laughing, I told her not to worry because I still had plenty of money. I was too embarrassed to let her know that I was broke.

The police pulled me over one day as I was picking up these gangster type guys that looked like they were up to something. They made them get out my cab, and gave me about five tickets for picking people up without the proper taxi license and registration. In New York, that's how taxis make their living. For some strange reason I remember how those two young detectives were looking at me. They were looking like they felt really sorry for me. They had seen the expression on my face like I couldn't afford those tickets. They also had that look like they knew I was just trying to make a living to survive. It was like they had to save my life that day and gave me the best warning that they could, encouraging me to find another line of work. It was just something about the way they looked that made me feel like something else was going on. I mean, sometimes you can feel certain things. And then, coincidentally, the tickets they wrote disappeared. They were never in the computer system and I never paid them. I never heard anything else about them and I am still curious about where those five tickets went!

The next day, I went to my friend, Henchmen's mechanic shop around the corner from where I lived. I complained to him about all the things I'd been through as a taxi driver and how I wanted to find the dude that beat me on his fare and break his jaw. He was a young punk with his pants hanging down. It hurt my pride to let a chump like that rob me. I was supposed to be "Big Un"! Henchmen told me to let it go and that I should be grateful he didn't kill me. I asked him if he'd teach me how to be a mechanic because I wanted to learn a trade. He agreed and told me he'd also pay me five dollars an hour but I never came back because I was stressed out about my trial, which was the following week.

CHAPTER 12: THE TRIAL

When it was time to go to trial for the "pawnshop robbery," Ernest's name was revealed. For a while, all the District Attorney used to say is that they had a secret informant. But when the trial started, Ernest went into hiding because he didn't want his identity revealed. We did not find out it was him until the trial was about to start. The District Attorney told him not to worry, because she was sure that we were going to cop out to the charges, and nobody would ever know who told them. But when she saw that we were taking things to trial, she revealed his name. That was her strategy to get him to come forward. She figured if we let him know we knew he was the secret snitch, he'd have nothing to lose and go on and tell his story. If he didn't tell, they were threatening him with perjury charges. Also, they knew he was an up and coming boxer with an undefeated record, and that he couldn't afford another arrest. Ernest had already served two years for burglary and was on parole. He recently caught another burglary rap one year prior to the case I was fighting. Ernest was on probation for a burglary he had recently committed so the D. A. threatened to charge him with perjury if he did not come forward. Going to jail, for him at that point, would have been a devastating setback for him and his management crew. He was almost near a title championship shot because he was undefeated with a 14-0 record.

I recall a day before the trial, while working out in Gleason's Gym two detectives came in, went into the office and spoke to Bruce Silverglade about the whereabouts of Ernest. He gave them information to the Tommy Gallagher Gym in Ozone Park in Queens. I assumed this is how they got the information. . I had never seen detectives come into the gym like that before. It was too much of a coincidence. I was peeking at them from across the ring when they came out of the office. One of the officers had a piece of paper in his hands. I knew what they were coming for because my trial was scheduled for the next day. Whenever the police are looking for a person to come to court who is not cooperating, they look for the person to subpoena them. Ernest made serious allegations and the D. A. needed him to testify because without him the case was about to be dismissed. I believe they subpoenaed Ernest right when they found him at that gym in Ozone Park, because when I saw his girlfriend parking by the court building, she was by herself so he must have been locked up in the courthouse waiting to testify. By that time, we knew who he was and we knew of his girlfriend. She grew up in the neighborhood with my crew. Also, Ernest's girlfriend had no other reason to be at the court house coincidentally on the same day that Ernest was subpoenaed and the trial was starting. I also knew that she had a habit of trailing him wherever he went. She was deeply in love with him and was anticipating him becoming a boxing champion. He had a lot of supporters and fans.

From the beginning of the trial, the judge was a mean ma'fucka whose name was Judge Greenberg. He had a reputation for being fair while presiding over cases but gave people the max if you blew trial. I came to court about ten minutes late, and he threatened that if I came to court late again, he'd revoke my bail. So from then on, I came ten minutes early. By the time the verdict was announced, the judge told me he appreciated how prompt and on time I was.

When Ernest came out to testify, he was smiling. The District Attorney was happy they had him, because that was all they had on us. He pointed to me, and said, "Yes, I recognize the guy that committed the crime. It's that guy right over there with the baldhead." He was trying to be funny, but when I testified, I got the last laugh.

My lawyer, who was replaced by another lawyer, named Michael Harrison, a strange guy who made weird faces. His personality consisted of making all kinds of gestures and facial expressions that were unusual to me. He also appeared to be a phony. He told me Ernest was burying me, and that I had no other choice but to testify. My back was up against the wall and I was furious when I took the stand. I was furious because Ernest actually had the audacity to try and put me away for a long time. After all we went through in the gym together training and sparring , him hanging out in my crib, me feeding him and lending him money, I felt double crossed! And to top it off, he made up a fabricated story just to convince the jury and the D. A. But I'd had sixteen months to think about this, and I'd written down my testimony. I was prepared for the District Attorney, and ready to counter attack what she would be throwing out. Mentally, I had anticipated over twenty questions I felt she would try to attack me with, and sure enough, all those questions I'd assumed she would ask, she did ask. But I was able to suppress all her ammunition and she ran out of bullets so to speak. I was answering questions like Bill Clinton did during his sex scandal with Monica Lewinsky. The D.A. said that I pretended that I was beating up the security guard like Hulk Hogan using a WWF tactic. The security guard was supposedly on the floor hollering, "Please don't hurt me! Please don't hurt me!" jerking and acting and playing it off.

She said Dembo was supposed to have been the gunman that told everybody to get on the floor and don't move. Cee allegedly was the bagman who put the gold in the bag, him and a Spanish guy that was a friend of the security guard. It was estimated to be $66,000 stolen. This was the D.A.'s closing argument, however, my lawyer objected and said the wholesale value was about $45,000. But yet, the owner of Gem filed an insurance claim for $66,000.

I was also supposed to have been the last one out of the store and locked the door from behind by taking the key from the front lock, and locking them in the store. It was a reversible key lock. That's how they concluded somebody from inside the store had to be involved with the hold up.

The security guard, Cisco, confessed the next day after the robbery, and he turned in his pal, the Spanish guy, who had just come from doing a five year bid as was later revealed in court. . The Spanish guy, Pedro, copped out to seven to life, and the security guard copped out to five to ten years. I was offered one and a half to four and a half years. Cee was offered two to four years. Dembo was offered the most time, a four to twelve year sentence! These guys were offered more time than I was because they all had prior felony convictions. We went to trial to fight the allegation and fight to stay free.

I exposed Ernest's reputation by using his prior arrest for burglary and robbery and tried to convince the jury that he was a liar. I told them that he had burglarized my locker and other lockers in the gym. I let them know there was a rivalry among us, and that Ernest was trying to capitalize off me by sending me up the river. I also told the jury that I wanted to harm him for robbing my locker but it wasn't worth it because I had a boxing career to pursue. I also told them that the reason why I conversed with the security guard was because I thought he might have seen me on MSG cable TV competing in the Golden Gloves. People would approach me all the time saying hey, "Weren't you the one on the Golden Gloves finals on TV?" Then I heard the judge whisper something about me and "guilt testimony" because it appeared like he knew I was winning over the jury.

I admit, I did use a few tactical techniques during my trial. You see, when you're out on bail, you get to see some of the people that's on your jury. You might find yourself eating right next to them in a cafeteria, or walking by them in the courthouse, or even riding up in an elevator while heading to court. You can't say anything to them, but you can indirectly give them messages through body language and gestures.

I came to court with my newborn baby, Rheavonni. I rode the elevator with a couple jurors that I knew were on my case. I held my baby on my shoulder and pushed close to one of the jurors, and put my baby right in her face. I wanted her to see what she'd be doing to this innocent kid if she let them convict me. My baby was very young at the time, and her breathing wasn't good because of the full elevator. She was breathing heavily, right in the juror's face.

I saw the expression on that lady's face, and from then on, I knew I had a shot at beating this thing.

I even tried to bring the baby inside the courtroom but the District Attorney got mad at the idea and my attempt to maneuver that she asked the judge to have the baby removed. The judge made Delores take the baby out of the courtroom.

I remained confident and patient, and really didn't care what happened because I felt my life was screwed up anyway. I even held the door open for the District Attorney and the police officer that arrested me when they came into the courtroom behind me.

The detective looked at me, and he saw that I had some kind of special confidence or something. It was a good thing that I used those tactics, because they were using tactics too. The police officers were lying through their teeth. They actually used a black officer, who wasn't anywhere around the scene, to say we drove up LaFayette Avenue. The way the street was designed, you couldn't even go that way from where the pawnshop was located. And one of the witnesses in the pawn shop said we went in a completely different direction. This guy was planted into the trial to help convict us and influence the African-American jurors. He was an "Uncle Tom" type of police officer that showed corruption was alive and well and because of officers like him innocent brothers are put into the position to be sent upstate to prison.

At the end of the trial, the judge was so impressed, he told me, "You're not guilty," even before they read the verdict. He appeared to be impressed by my competitive fight for my freedom.

As for the District Attorney, I sarcastically asked her after the "not guilty" verdict was read, "Can I have my girlfriend's jacket back?" They said I had used my girlfriend's jacket to cross dress after the robbery. My lawyer had made me put the jacket on during the trial, which didn't even fit. He made me try the jacket on like they did to O. J. Simpson on his trial. The D. A. was so disappointed that she had lost the case, that she started crying right in front of the judge. She looked like a fat insecure little girl who got her heart broken on a blind date.

As for my lawyer, when the verdict was read, I went to give him a quick thank you hug. He pushed my arms away, and said, "Oh, you don't have to hug me," like he was angry because I won. I mean, after all, the guy was Jewish, like the lady District Attorney, and he acted like he didn't enjoy her losing. And, I think, deep down inside he felt that I really was guilty. My thoughts were based on some of the things he had said to me. Anyway, it seems that most white people think that black men are guilty until proven innocent.

I felt he believed Ernest had been telling the truth, and he also respected him because he was an undefeated boxer with a 14-0 record. The lawyer was somewhat of a diehard sports fan. Unfortunately, I thought that the majority of white people believed that blacks were all criminals, so most of them were going to vote against us in court. I think the lawyer felt Ernest had some factual information about the robbery and besides, the D. A. did not care whether he was lying or telling the truth. They just wanted convictions. If the trial had been held in midtown where the jury would have been predominately white, I wouldn't have had an answer or a prayer. I was just grateful to have had some blacks on my jury that understood my culture and way of life.

For a black person, it helps a lot when at least half of the jury is black. That way you get equal opinions as opposed to an all white jury. History shows what happens to black men being judged by an all white jury.

When I came downstairs after the verdict, this white guy that was the foreman of the jury, shook his head at me and said, "Your speech and testimony is what saved you. "He said this as if to say they had wanted to convict me, but I had saved my own ass.

The foreman was letting me know that some people on the jury did not believe me. I had two counts against me, one for armed robbery in the first degree and the other for possession of stolen property. I was acquitted on the robbery charge but there was a hung jury on the stolen property charge. Eventually, it was thrown out. When I saw the black jurors outside, they all hugged and kissed me, saying, "Boy, you better stay out of trouble."

I felt like an emancipated nigga with another chance at life. I must admit that the trial straightened me out and taught me a valuable lesson. After that experience, I haven't committed another crime. That shows that a man doesn't always have to go to jail in order to learn how not to break the law.

In fact, if I would have gone to jail, I probably would have been worse off because I wouldn't have had a family or a career to follow and guide me to the light. I pretty much would've had nothing to live for, and that leads to self-destruction.

Now, I want people to understand that I am not glorifying my past criminal activities. I am just reflecting on my life experiences as a child on his way to becoming an adult. I feel like a victim of the messed up environment that I was born in. I strongly believe that stealing is a sickness, a disease I call "thievery". It is as addictive as any other habits such as drugs, cigarettes, sex and alcohol addictions.

Unfortunately, the government and people in general do not accept thievery as a sickness. They just automatically dismiss you as a bad person. They do not even take into consideration how this sickness develops. That is because the world is blind and unaware of this problem. Understanding thievery is sort of like learning new technology. It takes time but everyone needs to understand it. If the world can have empathy and understanding for people like Governor McGreevey and compassion for his "sickness," then why can't they have compassion for a man who is a thief and also has a sickness?

I think thieves need help and consideration too. It doesn't always have to be a jail cell. What about counseling? Some people need mental help. Some people need financial help. Drug dealing is also a form of thievery because dealers fuel their greed by selling illegal products to make money. Drug dealing is a disease and it falls into the same category as theft. So why does the government punish drug dealers more harshly, especially the non-violent ones? Look at the economic condition minorities' face. This is why plenty of people commit crimes. People need help so they develop this disease. I am not saying it is right but I do feel that people should get a fair chance to fight their disease because it is a serious problem like any other condition. This is why we have repeat offenders. And that is why it is a continuous problem, because it is not dealt with properly and in a civilized way. Statistics show that America is the number one country with the most people incarcerated. Next is China, then Russia. A lot of the other countries have alternatives before putting somebody in jail. It is documented in studies and articles and that is why their incarceration rate is lower than other countries.

The government is punishing crooks too harshly instead of trying to get to the root of the problem. First, they must understand the problem. Sending people to jail on a regular basis is not doing anything to cure the problem of drug dealing and robbery. In fact, it is just making matters worse because when thieves come home from prison, they usually do not have any support. They can't get a job and so therefore their disease goes untreated. If you notice, when a brother who comes home from jail, often he winds up right back because he was never cured. Some people try to combat the problem like any other addiction but without professional support it becomes a losing battle like the former New York Giant Lawrence Taylor said about his drug addiction. I have seen a lot of brothers who have come home and tried to overcome their addiction of thievery but failed due to the fact that everybody is so unaware and insensitive to their illness. They do not understand it nor except it the way that HIV was not accepted when it first began spreading. The brothers I know have gone on job interviews in which the majority of the time the company is owned by white men or represented by them. Black men are then automatically rejected from jobs due to their criminal backgrounds. Therefore, thievery is a cyclical condition which leads to increased drug dealing activity and rising robbery and murder rates. When is the government going to realize that robbery and drug dealing are diseases that start at a young age due to poverty? If three hungry dogs are together, what do they do when you throw a steak on the ground? They fight for the steak, right? Well it is the same way in the hood, in neighborhoods like the one I grew up in. Everyone is fighting to eat and survive. And sometimes murder is the result of this fight for survival. By creating more jobs and stopping the excessive punishment of people with these diseases, maybe it would help lower the murder rate.

I believe people should get counseling and proper medical help and attention for this dreadful illness I call thievery. One way to treat the disease would be to provide equal opportunities for employment for young people and provide them with jobs with decent medical benefits and a reasonable wage that keeps pace with inflation. Nowadays, people are working at jobs that are still paying the same wages as twenty years ago. Yet, the cost for rent, gas, food and every other necessity has increased. Do you think people are going to sit around while their stomachs are growling, look at that delicious fruit on the stand that they cannot afford and not try to steal it to overcome their hunger pains? The best solution in a case like this is for a business owner or employee who sees a hungry man like that is to quietly offer some fruit and show some consideration and help out the less fortunate. I mean, afterall, America is not Ethiopia. Doing something like that will make the world a better place for everyone to live together in peace and harmony because by feeding that man some fruit, you may have saved somebody's life that day or prevented something or somebody from getting robbed. And that goes for the people who are doing the hiring on jobs and in corporations as well. I believe these solutions are better than some of the solutions the government is proposing. For example look at the situation that took place at a New York City club one night. That White girl, Emette, was allegedly killed by the black bouncer at the club. Because of that one incident they want to now do a background check on bouncers. If you have a felony you cannot work as a bouncer anymore in New York City. Authorities know that approximately 80% of Black men who come home from prison, becoming a bouncer is the only job they can get. That means that over a million Black men will be out work because of one Asian/Hispanic girl.

I am not ashamed to talk about the sickness I inherited in my environment growing up because I know that I did not have a lot of control over the disease just like homosexuals do not have a lot of control over their sexual preference. Most gays caught that sickness at a very young age or they were born with it. To me, homosexuality is another form of sickness because God made Adam and Eve, not Adam and Adam or Eve and Eve and this disease is starting to spread at an alarming rate especially among women. Homosexuality has caused a devastating negative effect on society, particularly when you look at the spread of AIDS. What I understand from reading newspapers and other articles is that homosexuals were the first to spread the virus so therefore I am assuming this is where the problem originated from. Even so, the world can not point fingers at them and play the blame game nor hate them for their disease. Just as with thieves, society should not look at thieves with hate but instead embrace them and try to come up with a solution to solve the problem.

In the book, "Behold A Pale White Horse", the author William Cooper who worked for the government for many years, and allegedly died mysteriously, said that one of the government's plans was to give black men long prison sentences because they are the undesirables. The fact of the matter is, there are a lot of forms of thievery. Businessman who work for pharmaceutical companies are dishonest thieves. They are making counterfeit medications to sell to the sick. Stockbrokers give tips on stocks and cheat the shareholder. We got the Enron scandal. School administrators are regularly stealing from school funds. We also have medical thieves - people who are fraudulently committing insurance fraud. We have lawyers over pricing clients maliciously stealing their money. You have doctors treating patients for injuries that they know the patient does not have. Judges that buy their status is a form of thievery. These are all sophisticated forms of thievery that goes unnoticed and nobody really acknowledges or pays attention to it. You have businessmen in three piece suits camouflaging themselves because it is very difficult to tell that they are thieves by how they are dressed. People automatically assume that they are legit and that's the American way. So in reality we have thieves sentencing thieves and legislators who have homosexual backgrounds making laws. Former New Jersey governor, McGreevey has stated that there are a lot of people in government who are gay but refuse to come forward. The bottom line is being gay is a sickness and being a drug dealer and a thief is a sickness and disease but we just have to embrace each other, love each other and work with each other on a solution to the problem not by locking up and throwing away the key or gay bashing but finding legitimate help. Fortunately for me, I was able to cure my disease of thievery by becoming a salesman. Being a salesman gave me hope to survive and feed my kids without having to rob or steal from anybody.

CHAPTER 13: BUTTERBEAN KO'd

Meanwhile, I still continued to halfway train at the gym. For years, I still wasn't getting proper training from the trainers that I was still using. I was going from trainer to trainer and none of those guys were really teaching me anything that could improve my skills and conditioning. A lot of these trainers were just street hustlers who never really fought before. This trainer by the name of "Panama", showed me this boxing book called "How To Box" written by Nat Fleischer. When I saw the information in that book, I was amazed. I asked Panama if he could give me a copy so I could read it.

While reading the book, I was shocked at what I didn't know or wasn't taught as a boxer. It had all the techniques that a prizefighter needed to know. It showed how all the old time fighters trained and how they were supposed to eat. After studying that book, I felt a spirit of truth and possibility. I studied the lessons in the book like those Chinese fighters do in those karate flicks when they practice various techniques like the snake fist or the crane. I was determined to become a better and smarter fighter. For reasons that I do not know, I don't remember any of my previous trainers ever having a copy of this book nor did they ever suggest that I read it. I guess they couldn't because maybe they didn't know about it.

A couple of months later, me and this guy named Roosevelt, who was training me at the time, and I asked Bruce if he had a fight for me. Once again Bruce tried to set me up. He asked me whether I'd be willing to fight this up and coming boxer by the name of Butterbean at Madison Square Garden on December 15, 1995.

At first I was reluctant, then one day, my friend Erving told me that if I beat Butterbean I'd be real famous, and a lot of good things would happen to me. After that, I was convinced and told Bruce I'd take the fight.

I had five weeks to prepare for the fight, the longest I'd ever gotten to train for a fight. I was doing all the exercises from the book, and my trainer, Roosevelt, got so into it he wanted me to sign a contract making him my manager for four years. I didn't feel that was necessary, so we got into a dispute and parted ways three weeks prior to the fight. That left me without a manager or a trainer so I continued to train myself. But, while in the gym, a trainer by the name Joey Farriello, who trained Mark Breland, asked me if I wanted to make some money by being Buster Mathis' sparring partner and help him get ready for his fight with Mike Tyson. He even took me to camp with them. Farriello trained Breland who became welterweight champion of the world.

This was Mike Tyson's comeback fight after being released from prison. The fight was being televised nationally on Fox 5. We stayed at the Marriott Hotel in Philadelphia and trained in Joe Frazier's gym. At the gym, I was roughing Buster up so bad, I made it into the Philadelphia Daily News and they broadcasted me on the ABC affiliate WPVI TV Channel Six news that night.

When I made the news in Philly and told the media who I was fighting, somehow word got back to New York and people started calling Butterbean's top rank people. They told them they thought Ron Katz, the matchmaker, was making a big mistake by scheduling Butterbean to fight me because I wasn't what my record appeared to be. Even though my record was 1-6-1, they were telling Butterbean's people that I was a better fighter than my record represented. Those were rumors I had gotten from people in the fight game and around the gym but from what I understood, Butterbean couldn't pull out because he was getting paid good money and could not mess up the show at The Garden. So the show had to go on.

The morning of the fight, I was resting in my apartment, waiting for the biggest opportunity of my life. Somebody rang my bell, and when I looked out the peephole, I saw two white guys. When I asked who they were, one of the guys said they wanted to talk to me about the fight. They said something about having five big ones for me if I did the right thing tonight - lose.

I backed away from the door and darted to the back of the apartment. At the time I wasn't sure whether it was the police or the mob. I definitely didn't want any beef with the mob, because that was a man's worst nightmare. I also thought one of the guys might start busting shots through the door. I never said anything to them except when I first answered the door. Once I went into the back room, I never left until the two men disappeared.

I left to go to the Garden about five o'clock that evening. At the weigh-in, I saw the Malito brothers and a lot of other people that regularly attended fights. I also ran into a former sparring partner of mine, Lester" The Real Thing" Jason. He was joking with me that he was gonna break my legs with a two by four so he could replace me in the fight. He was aware of the publicity I'd get if I won the fight.

As I waited in the locker room, I watched fighters come back from their matches with busted eyes and noses. One fighter named Gerald Gray came back beaten and battered really badly. He was spitting up blood and everything which got me a little nervous.

That night was a big show because the main event was Oscar De LaHoya vs. Jessie James Leiya. Also on the card was Tracy Patterson vs. Arturo Gatti, plus Shannon Briggs vs. Mitch "Blood" Green. At the press conference, Bob Arum announced there was also a special championship match between Mitchell Rose and Eric Butterbean.

When it was finally time for me to come out, I was warm and ready. I had psyched myself up so much that I feared no man, and that I had two arms just like Butterbean and that we were going to go blow for blow and toe to toe. When I stepped into the arena, there were so many people looking on, I was absolutely amazed. I had hired some local trainers from Bedstuy Gym to work my corner. I brought George Washington and Lenox Blackmoore with me to the Garden.

When Butterbean came out, he got a big standing ovation from the crowd. When we did the face up, Butterbean looked me in the eyes as if to say, I ain't nothing but a nigga, and he was the superior master race. He glared at me with those big blue eyes and bald head looking like King Kong Bundy from WWF. He wouldn't blink which kind of sent shivers down my spine.

When the bell rang, it was time to fight and test my newfound confidence and improved condition. I had planned to execute the fight with my jab and keep Butterbean from coming in. People around the gym told me to use my jab. I saw how Butterbean would charge and rush at his opponents on cable TV.

In the first round, I kept jabbing his face and it started to work. It was like he fell right into my trap, like a rat or something, because he was eating jabs left and right. I had almost knocked him out by the end of the first round, and once the second round came, I was ready to finish him off. He continued eating more jabs, and then I started throwing right and left hooks that was taught to me by this old Italian trainer, Neil. That's when Butterbean knew I wasn't playing with him and started backing up. I saw the fear in his eyes, but at the same time, I saw the pride in his eyes. He refused to lie down for a nigga. In boxing, whenever there is a black fighter and white fighter in a fight, race is always a factor. It is sort of unavoidable. White fans scream "kill that nigga" and black fans say "fuck that cracker up." Boxing fans always make it a race issue. It's madness but it is reality. When Tyson bashed Lou Savarese's head in by reaching over the referee while he separated them in their fight, Lou surrendered like a punk, "Okay man. I give up. You got it." A lot of Italians and white people hated Tyson's guts for the whipping he put on Lou. And the Russians and Polish folks hated him even more when he broke Andrew Golota's jaw and made him damn near run out of the ring. The white boxing fans were pissed off at him for beating up those white boxers like that. I used to hear how they used to talk about Tyson and say offensive remarks. like "I can't stand that guy."

On this night at the Garden, the majority of the white fans were cheering for Butterbean. His outfit had the colors of the United States flag and his entire entourage wore it. I hit him with everything but the kitchen sink, but he still refused to lie down. As I was punching him, I was trying to put him down, but he wouldn't go for it.

After all those punches, I started feeling a little tired because my conditioning still wasn't that good. It was better than in other fights but still not really on a professional level. I did not realize it until after the fight. I thought that I was ready but I still wasn't. I virtually trained myself so my body wasn't pushed the way it was supposed to be.

When the referee stopped the fight in the second round because of the barrage of punches I was throwing, I said to myself, "Thank you Jesus." If the ref would have given us more time, I think Butterbean might've had a chance to come back, but with those wicked and crazy punches I was throwing, he felt it was the best thing to do. Butterbean's nose was bleeding, and he was stumbling all over the place. It appeared that he was in serious trouble.

After the fight was over, I was walking around the ring with my arms raised, popping trash talk. I saw George Foreman at ringside, and shouted, "Yo George, can I get a shot at your title?"

George just stared at me with those gleaming eyes, as if to say, Son, I'll kill you. Plus, George had just come off that stunning knockout victory over Michael Moore, so he seemed like he took it as a threat. We had direct eye contact, and George scared the shit outta me with his eyes. I turned away and continued celebrating with my corner men, Blackmoore and George Washington.

While I was celebrating, the arena was so quiet you could've heard a pin drop. I had never seen a crowd that quiet after a fight before and it was so satisfying, because all of my boxing career, people looked at me like I was a bum and I didn't get much respect from the boxing community. Only hardcore boxing fans in the gym knew I was a good fighter with a lot of talent.

Delores got to the fight late, but she was in time for me to flash her and my newborn baby, Rheavonni, right in the center of the ring. Everybody was watching, and I was letting them know I was a proud dad and a family man.

I was so happy when I saw Bruce Silverglade that I hugged him right in the middle of the crowd. I was trying to impress unity amongst people and businessmen. Bruce did not think paying me off was necessary because he knew that I was not a professionally conditioned fighter. Plus, he was the type of guy who did not want to get involved with anything that he felt could possibly jeopardize his business of owning a gym. Even though he used to send me out there to lose, I still appreciated the Butterbean fight.

Boxer, Lester Jason, asked me the next day why I hugged a Jew in front of all those people? I told him I loved all people, and he told me that Bruce wasn't my friend. The Malitos brothers, former police officers, also asked me the same question. They were the ones that confirmed to me that Top Rank wanted to give me five grand to take a dive. Top Rank Boxing is the name of promoter Bob Arum's company.

Bruce had allegedly told them not to worry, because I couldn't fight my way out of a wet paper bag. Plus, Bruce didn't want any part of such bribery, especially knowing the Malitos brothers were former police officers who were aware and present when the offer was being considered.

The following Monday after the fight, I went

back to Gleason's Gym dressed like a heavyweight champion. I wore a three-piece suit and tie, and everybody in the gym was smiling and congratulating me. Tommy Gallagher was there cheering me on, asking me to be Lou Saverese's sparring partner. Tommy Gallagher is a famous trainer who also participated in the the TV show "The Contenders." I was a respected fighter from then on. People showed me a lot of love and to this day, I'm still getting the same amount of love and respect they gave me ten years ago.

I was paid fifteen hundred dollars for the fight, while it was alleged that Butterbean got seventy-five grand. That was the most money a fighter had ever gotten for a four rounder, unless you were an Olympic Gold Medalist or a Great White Hope. They always paid white fighters more than black fighters. Promoters looked out for their own. It was rumored that he'd lost some lucrative endorsements and a couple of commercials as well. He was also scheduled to go on the David Letterman show but they canceled it, although Jay Leno later brought him on as a guest.

I remember watching the show, and Jay Leno asked Butterbean, "During your fight with Mitch Rose, did you feel like you had slipped in your own vomit?" In other words, he was trying to say, weren't you ashamed you had gotten beaten by a bum ass nigga like Mitch Rose?

People in the business were still trying to support Butterbean and to let him know that he was still the "Great White Hope." Essentially Butterbean's supporters wanted to reassure him that they still supported him regardless of the loss. The message they were sending was "Don't worry about that loss. We still have your back." At the Tuesday night fights, a boxing series that came on the USA cable channel every Tuesday night at 9pm, they crowned him the King of the Four Round Champ and they let him come out and show off his belt. The same one they hid from me after I beat him. It was rumored the belt was right on the table at the Garden the night of our fight, but when I upset him, they didn't bring it out. I never was given the belt even though I won the fight. But three months later when he fought again, they let him wear the belt and continue his crusade to stardom and fixed fights. I cannot say absolutely that Butterbean participated in fixed fights but any hardcore boxing fan could see that the guys that he was fighting did not have any boxing skills at all. They should not have been in a pro fight and it was obvious but they still found a way to put him in Playstation's "The Knockout Kings." And the thing about it was that Butterbean fought about forty opponents in this manner. The Tuesday Night Fights were held three months after our fight. I did not get the belt because it was designed for a white man to build confidence in the White culture. Boxing is corrupt and they make their own rules and regulations. I did not find out until a couple of weeks later. And I did not have any lawyer backing me up. I had no manager or promoter and everybody in the boxing industry's lips were sealed.

* * *

The fight with me and Butterbean was broadcast on HBO but cut out on the East Coast. The fight was tape delayed and they did not show it because of the upset I delivered. The point was to advertise him, not me. They were trying to make Butterbean a huge star that night. They showed it on the West Coast and some guy who claimed to be a rock star who I met at one of the boxing shows at the Garden sent me a copy of my fight with Butterbean. He said he was a fan of mine so he had no problem sending it to me.

When I received the tape and viewed it, I was amazed at how professional I looked. I also was amazed to hear Jim Lampley, George Foreman and Larry Merchant commenting on the fight. To me, Larry Merchant, was the best commentator since Howard Cosell but he made an insulting comment about me. He said they couldn't find a bad enough bum from Brooklyn that Butterbean could beat.

New York Post W.A. Funches Jr.

BUTTERBEANED: *Eric "Butterbean" Esch, 300-pound cult hero, backs away from right hand by Mitchell Rose last night at Garden. Rose scored only second pro win with TKO at 48 seconds of Round 2.*

BRIGGS WORKS QUICK

Scores 54-second KO; Butterbean squashed

By STEVE SERBY

THEY SAID: 'THROW

Charges fly as boxer adds punch to probe

By MICHELE McPHEE

LAS VEGAS — Promoters from Top Rank tried to bribe a Brooklyn boxer to take a dive in a 1995 heavyweight bout at Madison Square Garden, according to startling new allegations.

The boxer, Mitchell Rose, 34, told the Daily News he was offered $5,000 to throw the fight against Eric (Butterbean) Esch, but he refused to go down.

Rose, who since has retired, is cooperating with authorities leading a 20-month-long corruption probe of Bob Arum's Top Rank, one of the sport's biggest promoters.

"I was at my house just resting for the fight in the middle of the afternoon when someone knocked on my door. I looked out the peephole. There were two white guys from Top Rank who said they wanted to talk to me about the Butterbean fight," Rose told The News.

"They said, 'We have some money for you, a substantial amount of money.' They wanted me to take a dive. They didn't want me to beat Butterbean."

Rose said a promoter accompanied by a henchman offered him $5,000, on top of the $5,000 he would be paid just for getting in the ring.

DAILY NEWS EXCLUSIVE

At the time of the Dec. 15, 1995, fight, Butterbean was 14-0 and a fan favorite because of his "average Joe" persona and huge girth.

Rose was a virtual unknown out of Brooklyn's storied Gleason's Gym with one win and six losses on his record.

"That's why they wanted me to fight Butterbean. They saw me as just a bum who couldn't beat him. That's how Top Rank is. They wanted to find an easy target to pair with a rising star to build up their record," Rose said.

"Even if I wanted to throw the fight, I didn't trust those guys. I wasn't opening the door."

Rose knocked out Butterbean [illegible] seconds in[illegible] second round.

Mitchell Rose says he spurned $5,000 offer to take dive in 1995 fight against Butterbean (above). Brooklyn brawler Rose won by KO in second round.

BOXER BANNED IN PROBE

By MICHELE McPHEE
DAILY NEWS STAFF WRITER

A boxer suspected of throwing bouts has been denied a license in Indiana — becoming the second Top Rank promotions fighter to be barred from the ring amid a growing probe, the Daily News has learned.

Journeyman boxer Verdell Smith had been scheduled to fight on Friday in Indiana.

Instead, he's slated to spend the day being grilled by FBI Special Agent Henry Selumpf, who is overseeing Operation Match Book, a 20-month, wide-ranging, undercover probe of corruption in the boxing world.

The operation became public on Jan. 6, when the FBI marched into Top Rank's Las Vegas' office with a search warrant that cited intelligence gathered by an undercover NYPD detective posing as a New York mobster and an FBI agent posing as his muscle.

The investigators, who opened a bogus company called YGJ, which stands for "You're Going to Jail," had worked Smith's corner at a recent Top Rank-promoted fight against Dmitriy (Star of David) Salita.

Salita is an undefeated rising star in Top Rank's stable of fighters, and investigators believe his fight against Smith may have been fixed.

Smith is managed by former Top Rank matchmaker Sean Gibbons, who was fired by the company's head, Bob Arum, days after the FBI raid.

Both Smith and Gibbons have denied any wrongdoing.

Last week, Smith's attorney, Michael Marley, sent a letter to the Indiana Boxing commissioner saying his client has been unfairly blacklisted.

"They are barring this fighter because his name is coming up in this FBI case," said Marley, whose client's career record is 44-84. "Verdell Smith has no criminal record of any kind, and has not been accused of any crime."

Last month, another Top Rank fighter, Eric (Butterbean) Esch, was denied a license to fight in his native Alabama against an opponent, Wally Kienbaum, who had never fought professionally.

The denial came a week after ex-boxer Mitchell Rose told the Daily News that Top Rank promoters offered him $5,000 to throw a 1995 Madison Square Garden fight against Esch.

Rose has given his account to federal investigators.

Esch, known for his huge girth, has denied any wrongdoing.

Me with wife Delores and Vonny after victory over Butterbean, while his fans looked shocked over his defeat

Me with future Heavyweight Champion Shannon Briggs after victory over Butterbean

The Bean-Stalkers

THE MEN WHO WANT TO TURN BUTTERBEAN INTO SUCCOTASH

Matchmaker Ron Katz (below, center) was all smiles at the weigh-in for the Mitchell Rose-Butterbean bout, but he wasn't laughing later when Rose handed The Bean his only loss (right), via second-round TKO.

more real boxing experience. Mitchell Rose was someone who was ... and had never shown any real inclination to fight hard. I didn't know he had a Golden Gloves background. For The Bean, the guy trained as if he were getting ready for a world championship fight. Well, at least he went to the gym two days a week instead of one. And, not to make excuses, but The Bean wasn't himself that night. He got caught up in all the hype about fighting in New York for the first time."

So Katz went back to the tried-and-true formula that has been used successfully by every matchmaker seeking to puff and shine the records of heavyweight pretenders. You want to know how the likes of McNeeley and Vaughn Bean fraudulently obtained all those knockout victories? By going to the infamous tomato canneries in Indianapolis and Oklahoma City overseen, respectively, by Pete Susens and Sean Gibbons. They have a deep lineup of heavyweights who aren't exactly setups, but aren't likely to knock a promoted fighter's block off, either.

"You have to understand, Butterbean didn't come up with a regular background in boxing," Katz said. "He did all his fighting in Tough Man contests. So the level of his opponents was and is more in line with what you'd see in a Tough Man contest.

"Bruce and I basically call the same people when we're looking for opp-

CHAPTER 14: SELF PROMOTER

Although I became a boxing celebrity, I still had a difficult time obtaining a decent manager. A couple of people offered me opportunities and a trainer named Nate Boyd introduced me to a manager named Lenny Shaw. He offered me a decent fight against an opponent named Cory Smith with a decent amount of training time, but I was so paranoid, I didn't trust the guy. I thought he was trying to set me up like Bruce Silverglade had.

When I finally decided to accept the fight, I talked to Bruce first. Coincidentally, Bruce was very close with Lenny Shaw, so he told him something negative about me. When I went back to Lenny Shaw's office to talk about the fight, he told me he didn't know me and Bruce were doing business together and that he didn't want to cut Bruce's throat. So, he called off the business meeting where we were going to talk about him promoting me and instead refused to book fights for me. It was alleged that other people used to call the gym inquiring about me, but Bruce would tell them stuff like I wasn't in shape and that I was a lazy fighter. He used to tell people negative things just to keep me available in the gym for himself just to make matchmaking fees off of me by using me as an opponent for promoters. That's how he generated extra revenue to keep Gleason's Gym in business.

Eventually there was another big show at the Garden, and Bruce offered me a fight against my sparring partner, Gary "Bring the Pain" Bell. Knowing that Gary and I were cool and from the same gym striving for common goals, I didn't want to ruin his career. I stepped aside and let him fight on the show and enjoy the spotlight of fighting in front of over twenty thousand people.

The main event featured Lennox Lewis vs. Ray Mercer. That night felt like the end of my career. I felt like a jackass for not fighting Gary Bell on that show. It wasn't supposed to be about friends that night, but business. However, I did get to meet Holyfield that night. He was in the audience catching the fights.

We were in the elevator going out of the arena when someone said, "That's Mitch, the guy that beat Butterbean."

Evander said, "What? He beat Butterbean?"

I said, "Yeah, that's me, I'm the man."

He joked by saying that he wanted a piece of me. His manager, Dana Duva, was with him and also excited. He told me he wanted to speak with me about some fights. Holyfield and I went back to playing with each other. I hugged him with joy and excitement. He told me to handle my business first.

I exchanged information with Dana Duva. He told me he wanted to put me on the show called, The Young Heavyweights, which consisted of up and coming heavyweight prospects, Shannon Briggs, David Tua, Johnny Ruiz, who I also sparred with, and a variety of other prospects.

When he tried to make a bout, all the managers turned down a fight with me. None of them wanted a fight with me because I was considered a threat and a spoiler. Nobody wanted to take a chance at that time, and I assumed it was because of the devastation I did to Butterbean.

I had to wait six months for my next potential fight, which was against Shannon Briggs, who was coming off his first lost to Darryl "Doing Damage"

Wilson. We went into training for that fight but, within two weeks, the fight was canceled. I don't know what happened, but I heard that Shannon was still depressed over his loss to Darryl. Coincidentally, I had lost to Darryl earlier in my career. I fought Darryl in my third professional fight. I lost to him making my record 0-3.

Since the fight between me and Shannon didn't materialize, I was basically abandoned in the streets again with no direction, and not sure of where my next meal was coming from. I stayed hanging around the gym looking for another fight. After about a year, I still couldn't get a fight. Since I still did not have a manager or a promoter, a lot of managers would not risk their fighters in a bout with me. I started spreading rumors in the gym that Monte Barrett, an up and coming heavyweight, was afraid of me and didn't want to fight me. I told a main source intentionally so they'd go back and tell Monte. That's the way boxing is. Because I did not have any connections to try to hook up the fight, I had to go to the main source and agitate him into giving me a fight. I told Zab Judah, "Your boy is soft, he's ducking me." Zab told his brother, Daniel Judah, and Daniel approached me in Madison Square Garden at a fight and told me that I had lost my mind. He told me I was souped up from my fight with Butterbean and that Monte was gonna knock me out. I told him to tell Monte let's get it on.

Although Monte was my friend, I didn't care, I just wanted to fight, and I didn't care if it was an old lady. I was broke and my rent was due. Monte called the gym pay phone one day and asked me whether I was spreading rumors about him ducking me. He said he thought we were boys, and couldn't understand why I'd be challenging him. I told him business was business, and he told me he was going to tell his manager to put the fight together.

The fight was scheduled for four rounds. As for preparing for the fight, if you don't have backing, promoters are not going to let you get that much time to train. It's pretty much take it or leave it. If you leave it and decide not to fight at all, you will just continue to hang around the gym waiting like a club fighter. Monte's record at the time was 6-0 and mine was 2-6-1. I only had ten days to prepare for the fight, but I was trying to beat the odds even though I didn't have much time to train nor did I have a trainer.

A lot of people thought what I was doing was stupid but nobody wanted to say anything because they wanted me to lose and convert back to the bum they assumed I was. However, some believed I could win the fight. I came into the ring with an army hat and shirt on that read, "It's A Conspiracy Against Me" on the front, and on the back it read, "Mitch 'The Thug' Rose". I was trying to send the message that no matter what, as long as I was a black man, I would be looked at as a thug. I feel black men in society are just portrayed to have that image, especially among a predominately white crowd. It was also a feeling that I wanted to express. I also consider myself an entertainer and actor.

Monte was in such good shape that I said to myself, I'm in deep trouble. He was swinging hard wild punches that you heard in the wind. Knowing that he was my friend, and that I was wrong for even trying to take food out of his mouth, I couldn't even concentrate on winning. I was out to win but with ten days of training you can only do so much. I also could not get angry enough to hurt the guy. I did not take the fight seriously and I was joking the whole time just happy to be out in a boxing ring in front of a crowd. He hit me in the back of the head, the ear, chin, eye and then he busted my lip. I ended up having to get six stitches in my lip after the fight. I thank God I was talented enough to survive those four rounds without getting seriously hurt.

If the fight had been an eight or ten rounder, I would've been in a lot of trouble, possibly getting knocked out. But the fight was a four rounder and he won by decision. My friend, Joe Fogarty, was at ringside looking on and wishing me luck. Joe became a friend of mine after seeing me in the Golden Glove finals in 1988. Later on, he acted like a boxing manager by making calls to promoters all around the world trying to get me fights. The Judah brothers were in Monte's corner looking on laughing, stating, "I told him, I told him."

It was another lonely and unsuccessful night for me. Joe and I were losers again. I had sold myself down the river for a thousand dollars but I couldn't help it because I was desperate for money. After I paid the rent and a couple of bills, I was broke again. I didn't have any other way to make a living.

Monte and his family lived in the next building from where I lived in Linden Plaza. Every time I would see his wife and four kids, she was pleasant and would say good morning or hello to me. She accepted me as Monte's friend, but I wasn't trying to hear that friendship stuff any more in boxing. I felt that's what got me in the predicament I was in at the time.

CHAPTER 15: TRAVELING SALESMAN

Although the Butterbean fight was behind me, I still was cautious. I wasn't sure what was going to happen to me, I thought someone was going to assassinate me. Butterbean was promoted by powerful people in boxing and he was a stone cold redneck from Alabama. He was the great white hope and with the rumors about boxing and mob ties, I wasn't sure what was going to happen. A lot of people joked about how I had better be careful. Some people were serious about the situation.

I was at Bedstuy Gym one day talking to James Davis. He used to come by and visit often and he was joking about how I'd better watch out for Butterbean's people who might want to kill me. This guy was a police officer at the time so I was pretty nervous. I loved boxing and appreciated my accomplishment and I was willing to accept death if it occurred. I had been boxing for over ten years and boxing was like my religion. It's what helped me to start thinking positively and striving for some kind of success. And it helped me to overcome drugs and kept me healthy. It is not always about being rich and famous. My sanity was more important. I knew I would be giving my life for a cause and my dream so I didn't feel bad, because like Martin Luther King said, "if you don't have a cause to die for, you might as well be dead."

Fortunately, years later I'm still here and my fans are still with me and loyal. They are constantly asking me to get a rematch with Butterbean. I was hearing it so much I had to do something about it. Since I didn't receive the belt that I was entitled to and Butterbean was making up excuses for why he lost, I wanted to give him a rematch. I wanted to test his heart and see if he was willing to redeem himself. When I made some money years later, I decided to try and promote a rematch.

I had flyers made up, t-shirts pressed and a website posted. I paid workers to pass out flyers at fights all over New York and I littered Madison Square Garden with the flyers. Some people thought I was foolish while some thought it wasn't a bad idea. It started getting expensive and I felt like I was at a dead end because Butterbean just wasn't interested in fighting me again.

In 2002, I caught up with him at his fight against Larry Holmes at the Virginia Scope Arena. I went all the way to Virginia, looking to start trouble with the guy. I wore a Ku Klux Klan outfit as a gimmick. I walked around the arena posing and taking pictures with the audience. I wanted to get in the ring when it was over, but was nervous because I thought the police would lock me up. Virginia was a commonwealth state like Alabama, and wasn't as lenient as New York laws were. So instead, I stayed back and waited at ringside.

When the fight was over and Butterbean and his entourage were coming out of the ring, I shouted, "Yo Butterbean!" He looked at me. I told him he was a fake and a fraud, and that he was deceiving people. I also told him I'd knock him out again and even faster this time. He just stared at me in shock and fear before walking away with his entourage in tow. That was the end of my crusade, but I'd been able to get the anger off my chest for cheating me out of the King of the Four Round belt and lowballing me by paying me $1,500 and paying him $75,000. I felt a big release and satisfaction. Unfortunately, I didn't get to grab any media attention or press. The stunt failed publicly but personally and emotionally, it was a winner.

It was now time to start looking for other things in my life to do besides boxing. The first thing you'd think I do was look for a job. Well, for me, jobs weren't easy to find, so I went back to the only place I knew, Midtown. I was contemplating robbing somebody until I ran into my old friend named "Cee God." When I told him what my intention was, he told me I needed to be ashamed of myself for thinking such nonsense.

As I walked around Midtown with him, he told me things that made me think. He talked about being home for my family, and being too old for that same mentality. I was twenty-eight years old, still with Delores and had two kids. He took me to spots where you could buy wholesale watches, clothes and costume jewelry. He brought me a couple of watches and showed me how to sell them. His goal was to show me how it was done but after two days, he left me on my own to fend for myself.

I was still inexperienced, so after two weeks, I was a shy salesman that didn't know how to accept rejection. I went back into a depressed state and started, once again, contemplating about robbing someone, but instead I went inside this deli restaurant and hung out with the Mexicans on their lunch break at 34th and 8th Avenues.

The Mexicans I knew eased their pain with a couple of beers, so I opted to drink a couple myself which gave me a new sense of courage. I went back outside with a more aggressive approach and started selling my watches like crazy. I didn't care about the cops or anybody, it was all about survival. About two months later, I ran into my man, Mike, a brother I met in Brooklyn at the barber shop, who ultimately showed me the vending game. He put me on to designer shades and other profitable products. He also showed me other places to sell merchandise, which were more convenient and active, with less hassle.

I got so deep into selling merchandise that I started traveling all over to sell my products. I went from Atlanta to Oklahoma and then all the way to England. Being a salesman gave me a sense of survival and hope. Hope to own my own business one day. And hope to always have food on the table for my family.

It was unfortunate that the police were locking up brothers for selling watches and clothes, and then were taking their products. They would not give us a license unless we were veterans. I believed that being a salesman deterred a lot of crime. But it seemed like the system was always attacking brothers that found a way to make a living. I thought it was the American dream to own your own business. Brothers have got to become entrepreneurs in this society because we're still being treated like underprivileged workers with low wages. The system refuses to pay us equal to what white people earn and that's what Dr. King died for in his last mission.

I knew I had to make a way for me and my family, and I was the type of guy that had big dreams and wanted the best things in life so I hustled. I used to walk forty or fifty blocks, sometimes seven days a week, selling merchandise. I would approach hundreds of people a week, trying to persuade them to buy my product. I still had that saving mentality since I was a young kid, so I knew how to stretch my money.

I was able to save over twenty thousand dollars in two years as a salesman, with the help of my wife,

Delores, whom I married in 1999. She had been working for over fifteen years, and I always made sure she saved money because we always talked about having our own business and a big house one day.

Together with my wife's savings and gifts from our wedding, we had over one hundred thousand dollars saved up, and it was time for us to start looking for an investment. I began to look for a business opportunity where I wouldn't lose our money. One day while riding down Utica Avenue in Crown Heights, Brooklyn, I stopped by an old friend's printing shop. He had bought the whole building, which also had four commercial stores. One was a vacant liquor store, and I asked him if I could rent that store. He agreed to give me the opportunity to try running my own business.

Errol Robinson, a Jamaican guy was one of the few people that had ever given me an opportunity to try and succeed. I took full advantage of that opportunity. I built the store up to a mega store. I used only twenty thousand of my wife's and my savings to open the store. Two years later, the store was worth 1.3 million. I had finally got a piece of the rock.

My customers loved and respected me, and the majority of them called me "Champ." The whole neighborhood knew who I was. I hired an artist to paint pictures on the gate of my store, pictures of all the great black athletes. I had Muhammad Ali and Laila Ali, Roy Jones, Holyfield. I even had Mike Tyson. I had Tiger Woods, Malcolm X, Serena and Venus Williams, Jackie Joyner, Carl Lewis, and of course, me. I had Jack Johnson who was the first black heavyweight champion in boxing who was known for his larger than life personality, carrying a bottle of

Jack Daniels in his jab. People in the community loved the art and loved me for advertising such prominent sport figures in the neighborhood for the youth to envision and emulate. The store was so successful, I started to party and drink in excess.

I bought a $60,000, 2002 Cadillac Escalade, then a $6,500 Rolex watch. I bought a mink coat that cost over five grand. I started hanging out more partying and enjoying my new found success. This was all thanks to Mr. Robinson, a black business property owner, who gave me an opportunity to excel. Unfortunately, when I tried to lease a couple of other stores to do business it was really difficult because the property was owned by Jews or Arabs and most of them seemed like they did not want to rent to me. It was if they had something against a young black male. It is as though they automatically thought I was going to sell drugs or conduct illegal business on their premises. I would have to be P. Diddy or Denzel Washington to get a lease out of these people. And this is the reason I think a lot of black males do not have businesses - they can't get a lease.

From my experience of being a businessman, I can say that it is very rough out there for black men and it can be discouraging and aggravating. My store was making so much money between liquor sales and lottery sales that when I went to the bank to make my weekly deposit, the bank tellers were watching me suspiciously, eventually reporting me to a manager. This black lady manager at Chase actually called me up and asked me why I was making irregular deposits by putting in eight thousand dollars or nine thousand dollars at a time but never going over ten thousand dollars. When I started banking in Long Island, those white people started reporting me to the police and every official they could think of. When I eventually went to apply for a gun permit for protection, the black, female police officers who were in charge of issuing the permits laughed me all the way out of One Police Plaza even before doing any kind of background check. They were mocking me and teasing me and imitating the way that I spoke and warning me ahead of time that I was not going to be able to get a gun permit. Yet, I was seeing young Jews, Arabs and Koreans coming out with gun permits. I thought to myself, "America ain't no place for a black man." Black men are denied the right to bear arms but yet the Arabs got the majority of the delis throughout all of New York City. Therefore we are surrounded but cannot defend ourselves nor our country. And the scary part about it is that they have the most dangerous assault weapons that you can imagine. You go up in their stores and you see them posing in pictures with machine guns, M16s and every other rifle you can imagine. This is an example of how fucked up the government is. And it is this type of thing that makes the Koreans keep begging for war with America. It's like we are supposed to just lay down and die for the enemy. How could they deny people gun permits as violent as America is? How are we supposed to help defend the country with this stubborn racial bullshit going on in "America?" The enemy is going to wipe this country out if we don't change our evil hearts towards the black man. Not having a self defense law is the most ridiculous atrocity I have ever heard of. Not only do we have to worry about the brothers and Aryan nation and hellraisers but the Arabs too. So imagine how vulnerable a man like myself feels. I felt like a cow waiting to be slaughtered.

All of these things frustrated me to the point that I wanted out. I had family members and friends who worked for me, but were stealing my merchandise from the liquor store. I was losing money. I went deep into a hole because I often wasn't watching my store because I was busy running my other business, a mechanic and auto body shop. I decided to bail out and sell my liquor store business. I sold it for somewhere around six figures, a fraction of what is was worth. I closed down the gates, wrote a screenplay called "The Liquor Store" then started a lingerie line called Katrina's Diary. Then I went back to the gym.

Posing with former Middleweight champion Thomas "The Hit Man" Hearns, #1 contender Devalle and Gerald Gray

CHAPTER 16: STREET FIGHT WITH MIKE TYSON

One late night while hanging out about three o'clock in the morning, I went to a local neighborhood club called Sugarhill. It's a spot where you see the regular partygoers and people from school or around the hood that you haven't seen in years. I was walking around the club laughing, mingling and dancing having a good time. As I proceeded to go and buy myself another round of Hennessey, out of the blue I saw Mike Tyson sitting next to the bar so I walked over to him and said hello. I knew that a lot of celebrities in situations like this can be anti-social and sort of leery of common people but I figured it was alright to say "what up" to Mike because I had met him a few times before including one time back in 1987 while I was in Midtown in Macy's scheming on the F.I.L.A sweat suit that I was trying to shoplift.

When I saw him at Macy's I said "What's up brother?" He responded, "What up dawg?" We shook hands and he continued shopping heading to a counter with a bunch of sweatshirts and shirts. Teasing me, he flashed a stack of one hundred dollar bills to pay for his purchase. I'm pretty familiar with stacks so I estimated it had to be about ten thousand dollars he pulled out. And this was when he was only 15-0 as a pro so he was not as popular then. The thought flashed through my head, can I rob this dude? But then I thought to myself, "Man you must be crazy. Look how tough and crazy this guy looks." Besides, I did not rob brothers. However, I also thought about asking him can I be his sparring partner but I was too proud to beg. Years later I regretted not asking him because you never know, he might have given me a chance.

Eventually, I met him again years later in Philly at the Marriott Hotel when I was Buster Mathis's sparring partner. This was when Mike Tyson and Buster were scheduled to fight on Fox 5 live. It was to be Mike's comeback fight after being incarcerated for rape. He was always a pleasant guy to me and kept it real. At the Marriott, he pulled up in front of the hotel and jumped out of a brand new500 Benz. Right in back of him was his entourage in five more brand new s500 Benzs. I was standing in the lobby looking out the window saying to myself, "God damn. Why can't I get on like this guy? I'm up here like cattle sparring for five hundred dollars a week." When he came through the door, he looked right at me and I said, "What's up champ?" He said "What's up player?" and proceeded to go to his destination. I stood around the hotel front desk with some of the desk clerks, all women. They looked excited to have seen Mike Tyson and I was feeling like a broke ass boxer!

Mike never seemed to look down at people and it seemed like he did not forget where he came from. He tried to say hi to as many people as he could. That's why I said hello to him at Sugarhill. When he spoke to me at the club, I asked him if he remembered me. It was dark inside the club and he gave me that look of confusion, as if saying who the hell are you? So I tried to refresh his memory by saying, I'm Mitch Rose, the guy that knocked out Butterbean. I said that because that was my claim to fame. A lot of people know me from that infamous knockout. Boxers especially knew about that fight.

For some reason, Mike got a little hostile by my statement and said, "Man, come on with that. I don't want to hear that bullshit." I started laughing and said

"Okay man." I then started gesturing with my hands, waving them to indicate that I did not want any confusion or static. We continued talking and socializing and then all of a sudden Tracy Morgan, who was also a comedian on NBC's Saturday Night Live walked by and saw Mike. He came over and started joking with us telling Mike how much he loved and admired him. He was so emotional about meeting Mr. Tyson that he got on his knees waving his hands like he was praying to Allah or some god. He told Mike that he was willing to kiss his feet because he's the messiah of boxing. Mike was just looking and smiling wondering what this guy was talking about. He seemed not to have a clue who he was. Mike thought he was a junkie because he had the carved out cocaine straw in his ear and his nose had dried up residue that was either cocaine or heroine. I started laughing again explaining to him that Tracy was the famous comedian who played the character "Hustle Man" on the Martin show.

After that incident, one of Mike's "hanger ons" came over to the table and pulled out about an ounce of weed. I looked at Mike and said "Wow, y'all niggas got the goods." He turned around and said, "Yo dawg, you want to smoke a blunt with me?" I said "You motherfucking right!" I mean, after all, I had been wanting a puff of weed all night.

So Mike was right on time. I even pulled out a pack of bamboo and said "You need this?" Mike said, "Man, put that bullshit away if you want to puff with me. " It was as if he knew that I was craving for some trees that night. He continued to say that if you want to puff with me, you can't be pulling bullshit out like that. He was kind of treating me like I was a dope fiend or something. I just shrugged it off and said, "You got it brother." He then said that his people were going to the store to get a blunt so I should chill and lay low.

Later on, we all got up and went on the dance floor to mingle and socialize a little. Soon, Mike grabbed a slim shorty and was rubbing her from behind with his dick up against her butt. Then he started squeezing her ass aggressively on the dance floor. It was almost like he could not dance so he substituted that lack of ability by squeezing her up like a stripper or rag doll. Mike was wearing tight black highwater pants, shiny black shoes and a khaki shirt with suspenders, looking like a muscle bound Michael Jackson without the jheri curls. I was just standing near laughing in amazement saying to myself that this guy is tripping Brooklyn style. I then walked off and found a young lady and took her on the dance floor and got down like John Travolta on Saturday Night Fever.

When I finished dancing, I walked back to the table and Mike was sitting all alone puffing on the blunt. I sat next to him and said "Puff and pass nigga." He passed me the blunt and it felt like a beautiful thing to puff on a blunt along with the most exciting boxer of all times. Growing up in Brooklyn, I have puffed blunts with a lot of people but it was the ultimate to puff with Mike. While we were smoking I asked him if he wanted to go downstairs to get out of the public eye because everybody was staring at us smoking up the place. Sugarhill was a club where nobody could get away with smoking in the open like that but Mike had that power and privilege. He said "fuck that" to Sugarhill's smoking policy, "We puff right here." I said to myself, "Excuse me." I was thinking about the twenty million dollar fight Mike had coming up in six months against Lenox Lewis. I said to myself,

"Lenox is going to whip Mike's ass but Mike is going to laugh all the way to the bank." I guess Mike was celebrating being on top of the world again. We were blazing back and forth all night. I was having so much fun that I started doing stand up comedy making Mike laugh his ass off.

I have to admit, I was being a little flashy, showing off my Rolex and standing tall in my $5,000 three quarter mink coat. I knew I couldn't compete with Mike and the money he had but I was happy I was not a complete bum with nothing. I had a hundred thousand dollars in the safe deposit box and my 2002 Cadillac Escalade was parked outside waiting for me.

I was not intimidated by Mike and his success. In fact, I was proud to be hanging out with him for that period. I definitely was not feeling like a woman looking to get money out of him. I am a man and I believe all men have to fend for themselves. As a fighter, it might have crossed my mind to be able to go to camp with him to study some of his training methods.

Eventually Mike's friend, Arum, the son of the owner of the club, started harassing me by saying, "Yo man, Mike has to have some privacy." He wanted to break up our party for some reason. He appeared to be envious of our connection. I think Mike and I got along so well because we came up doing a lot of the same bullshit as kids. We were both boxers and shared a lot of the same views.

I eventually decided to bailout because the day was breaking and it was time to move on. Besides, I did not want to keep hanging around him like I was a groupie or something. I decided to bounce without going over to say farewell. I stood outside the club for a few minutes then I jumped into my truck feeling drunk and high as a motherfucker. As I drove a block away, I said to myself, "Nigga, you too drunk to be driving." So I drove around the block and crept back in front of the club to pass some time and mingle with club goers and the ladies. I double parked across the street. Coincidentally, Mike Tyson came out of the club at the same time that I had decided to get out of my truck to socialize with the crowd out front. But before I got out, I waved to Mike as I tried to show off my brand new Cadillac that I had just bought four months prior. Mike just started laughing saying "this guy." I walk over to give Mike a last farewell handshake because I knew the chance of seeing him anytime soon was slim. I wanted to tell him peace and take care. I also wanted him to know that I appreciated the smoke and him laughing at my jokes but unfortunately, when I have liquor in my system I tend to say things that sometimes hurt people's feelings.

As Mike was walking to the waiting limousine with the girls we were hanging out with in the club, it was just an involuntary reaction to say something about the situation. Knowing Mike's past history with women and the trouble he had been in, it dawned on me that he could possibly be heading for self destruction again so I shouted out, "Yo Mike, be careful with those chicken heads. " To be honest, I did not know exactly what a chicken head was. I knew that it was a phrase people in the hood and on rap videos would use. But I did not know the phrase would offend Mike the way that it did.

The statement came out pretty loud so the crowd outside the club began instigating a fight like the way they used to do in the parks in Brooklyn back in 1979. You heard a chorus of "whoas" by about ten people. I was smiling and backing up saying "Mike, chill. " I did not want any static and I was simply trying to get him to relax. Mike looked at me with an angry look and he kept staring at me. I still continued to back up trying to avoid a confrontation. I was trying to gesture as if to say that I did not mean anything by what I said but Mike decided to surge forward, like Mighty Joe Young, screaming and shouting and saying to me, "You a disrespectful ma'fucka man!" He continued to charge forward until about four security guards grabbed him and restrained him from attacking. Mike acted like he was calming down pretending to go to the limo but as they let him go, he made a quarterback football player move and ran around the security guards and followed me into the middle of the street. I guess he was expecting me to run or scream like a girl but I didn't. He threw his hands up and said "What's up now ma'fucka? You talking all that shit. He got in his crunch position, steps his right foot out to have balance and leverage to knock me out. I was surprised, drunk and I had on slippery shoes so I was not sure what was next. As he began to let off his ferocious hooks, the security guard grabbed him and you could hear people saying "No, your gonna kill that guy".

Although they grabbed him, somehow Mike still was able to clutch my arms before I got away. His speed was like a cat catching a rat! We were wrestling and I was saying to myself, "Oh my God. I have got to get away before he unleashes a hook while holding me by the arms." I started getting flashbacks from when I used to be in Midtown breaking away from the police so I slipped out of my coat to get loose from Mike's tight grip. In the process of backing up, I lost my balance and fell to the ground injuring my elbow and neck. I hit the ground very hard because I weighed about 275 pounds. I had not been in the gym in years, just occasionally to exercise and visit. I had just been hanging out drinking myself into oblivion. A security guard from the club, who I knew from the neighborhood helped me to my feet.

As I stumbled across the street, Mike walked and picked up my mink coat off the ground and then started ripping it up like a wild man. Mumbling, he was saying "You punk ma'fucka you" as if he had something against my coat. And he knew it was a pretty motherfucking coat too. While we were in the club, he saw how the ladies were giving me more attention than him. They were treating me like I was the star! I believe he was jealous of me and my coat. I got so mad when he tore my coat up that I ran to the truck looking for a pen to write down the license plate number of the limo he was riding in. The security guard beside me thought I was going for a gun. As I reached into my glove compartment, he said, "Hey, what are you getting man?" but I was only looking for a pen to write down the license plate number. I did not want Mike to get away and later be able to deny the claim. After I got the plate number, the limo sped off with Tyson and the three girls who were in the club. I just stood in the middle of the street mad as a motherfucker. Then I saw my mink coat on the ground looking like a dead animal. In a daze, I turned and saw the crowd looking stunned and amazed. Some began to laugh. Then I decided that the right thing to do was to call the police as well as an ambulance. I thought to myself, "I could do this like a law abiding citizen or a nigga from the streets."

When the cops arrived, I showed them my mink coat on the ground in front of the club and I was shaken up as well. When I mentioned it was Mike Tyson that attacked me, they started kind of shying away from the situation telling me that a police report was not necessary. I said, "What the fuck do you mean a report is not necessary? Who is going to pay for the damage to my coat? I insisted that a report be done. They continued to refuse to write one so I had to bluff them to get them to do a report. I called my lawyer while sitting on the backseat of the patrol car. I put it on speakerphone so that they could hear his voice. When the two young black police officers heard that Jewish voice, I heard one of them whisper, "We better go ahead and do the report." Then I told them to send me an ambulance while you are at it because my back and elbow was hurting. When the ambulance arrived, I told them what happened and they started to treat me, although reluctantly. They made it seem as if I was faking my injuries. I told them that I did not want to hear anything and to just take me to see a doctor. They were two Spanish EMTs who were eventually interviewed by the D. A. after my lawsuit against Tyson was filed. The EMTs told the D. A. that I was wasted and that my breath smelled like liquor.

It seemed as though everybody was defending Mike Tyson for his actions. Even the doctors tried to aid Mike in not getting prosecuted. I did not know this stuff immediately but I found out when my lawyer read the hospital report to me. The doctors mentioned to the D.A. that I told them that Mike and I were drinking and smoking together. They also said that my injuries were exaggerated. I believe that was a malicious accusation and a way to protect Mike.

They were not concerned about my health. They only assumed that I was trying to get money out of Mike. It was as if it was okay to get attacked and have your property destroyed by Tyson. I could not believe how everybody was playing superhero to defend Mike.

When my wife came to pick me up from the hospital, she was in shock and had a bewildered look on her face. I told her that I would be alright. She drove us home and when I awoke later that evening, I was still heated and angry over the fact that the police did not want to make a report and that the doctors acted like they did not care about my health. That was when I decided to call the Daily News about this story. When I told one of the reporters, he took my name and number. About an hour later, the Daily News called. Then the New York Post called, followed by the New York Times. They all wanted the story. Since news outlets have their connections, Channel 4 news called my house. A reporter named Kendra Farm called and was very enthusiastic about doing a Mike Tyson story. Kendra was a beautiful, flashy white lady who wore sparkling diamonds in her ears, around her neck and on her fingers and wrists. She told me to stay put, that she was on her way. She was at my house in a flash. The channel 2 news came unexpectedly. I felt like I was getting interviewed for a heavyweight championship fight with Mike Tyson with all the press and media exposure.

Kendra Farm asked me if I had any proof of my fights in the past. I gave her a copy of the Butterbean fight. It was a good thing I had tapes lying around from the rematch promotion I had done. She aired the tape live on Channel 4 News. My promotion was finally paying off. I had revived the fight with me and Butterbean. It was something that I wanted to keep alive so that people would not forget. That fight was the greatest four round fight of all time. The fight received an extraordinary amount of media attention. I still get respect from that fight like the Thriller in Manila whether people like it or not. Mike Tyson just gave me better leverage on my promotion with his antics that night at the Sugarhill Club. The Tyson street fight looked so sweet that the District Attorney thought I had staged the entire thing.

The detective called me up to interview me and I went down to the police station with a neck brace on that I got from the hospital and explained what happened. I spoke to a Spanish officer by the name of Detective Lasada. He was a cool cop who appeared to sincerely want to help me with the prosecution of Tyson. But I told him a lie. I said that the truck I was in was a green Expedition instead of the white Cadillac Escalade that I was in. I felt that if I mentioned the 2002 Escalade, they would probably be too curious on how I purchased a sixty five thousand dollar truck, so I tried to avoid that. I felt uncomfortable speaking to the police about my business because they usually look at all black men as criminals. The sergeant, a short white guy named Detective Gallagher, did not seem like he wanted to do too much. Plus, witnesses were afraid of Tyson's entourage so they did not want to tell what happened. There were about fifteen witnesses standing outside when it happened. Three eventually came forward but for some strange reason, they backed out too. So in the eyes of the DA and the police, I was a liar.

It seems as though if a young black male reports a crime committed against him, nine times out of ten, that black male will be investigated as well because the police are very suspicious of them. Most of them don't like black men nor trust them. But the truth of the matter is, the police are human and do a lot of criminal bullshit too. Black men are afraid of the police because of all the malicious shooting they do to unarmed brothers. People are not stupid and they know that it does not take 41 shots to restrain or stop a person. Boxers get swung at all of the time so when they hear of a cop shooting a guy 20 feet away for holding a pipe or even a knife, we think it is ridiculous. These shootings are deliberate acts of hate and trigger happiness.

The precincts in New York are like the precincts in the movie Mississippi Burning - you have no help. The law is not on your side. Basically, that means you are pretty much on your own. That is why brothers go and handle their business on their own in the streets. If I would have gone that route, I would have been a dumb nigger. I tried the law abiding citizen way and I was made out to be a snitch and a gold digger, so I'm damned if I do and damned if I don't.

When I called the District Attorney's office to find out what they were going to do about my property and injury, I was told the head District Attorney in charge was on vacation in the Bahamas. This reminded me of the same shit that was going on in the book that I had read about Jack Johnson, the first black heavyweight champion of the world. He was paying the District Attorney's office and sending them on vacation when he got into trouble.

Man, I was so pissed off about how they were trying to cover up everything for Tyson. I went to the press conference for the Mike Tyson/Lennox Lewis fight with a Batman and Robin-type mask on. I drank a bottle of E&J Brandy and with a fake ounce of weed in my Versace suit pocket. I stood on the balcony waiting for Mike to come on stage so that I could tell him how I felt about what he had done to me. I wanted to tell him to his face in front of everybody but they would not let him come out until they escorted me out of the arena. As they proceeded to escort me out, I made a deceptive move like Mike when he tried to get at me in front of the Sugarhill Club. I played it off like I was cooperating with them by leaving but as I pretended to walk up the steps, I reversed and ran to the balcony and began shouting my feelings that I had rehearsed in my mind about things I wanted to tell Mike. The security guards waited to let me finish my speech. Cameras began to flash from all directions. It was the most beautiful event I have ever seen in my entire life. It was like I was performing live on Broadway at the Millenium Hotel. I was waving my hands up in the air preaching my story.

I shouted that Mike was a faggot and liked to get fucked in his ass and that his wife needed a real man like me. I said that the people knew who I was. I was the man that fucked up that Great White Hope Butterbean and that I would fuck Mike Tyson up too. Then I began my demonstration and pulled out the fake bag of weed and threw it into the crowd of the press while the cameras were still rolling. After I finished my speech, the security guards and the police escorted me out of the hotel. I felt a big load off of my chest even though I knew that my stunt would be incriminating to my case. But I figured that they were not going to do much anyway. So I went and put on a show while I was still a hot topic.

Once again I made the newspaper headlines. Vic Siegel got the exclusive and gave me a nice story in the sports section of the New York Daily News. I also believed I saw the Regis & Kelly morning show with Kelly showing the article to her television audience. She said "Way to go Mitch! Great work!" I thought it would get more airplay but Mike stole the show by biting Lennox Lewis on the leg in that famous melee at the press conference.

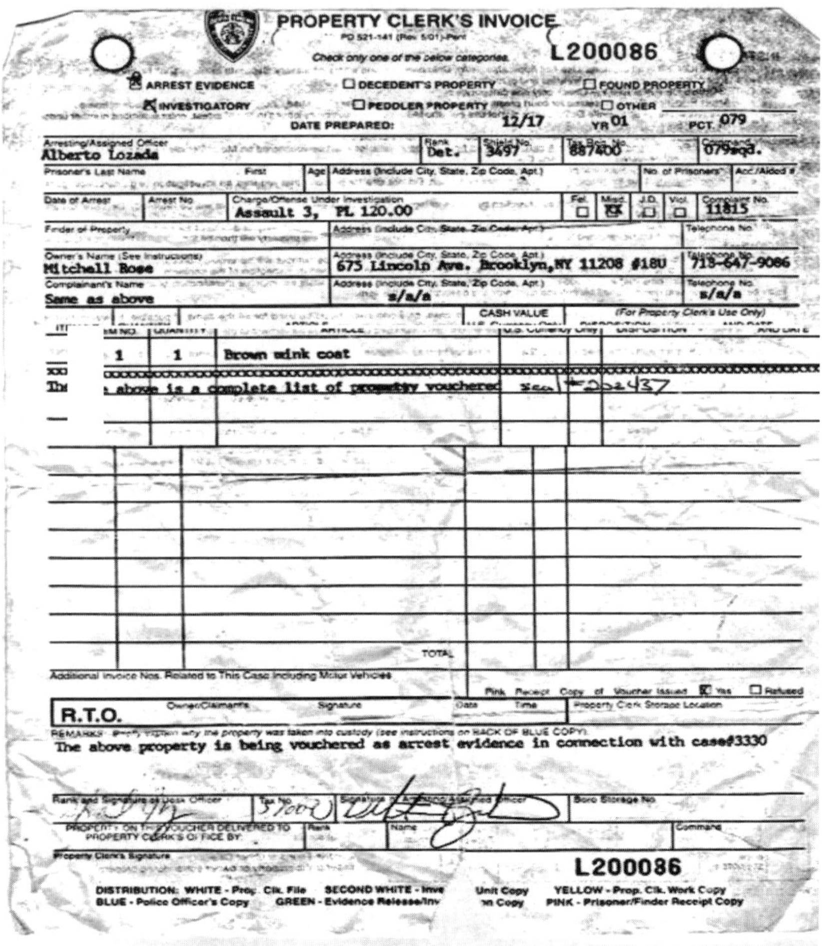

PROPERTY CLERK'S INVOICE
PD 521-141 (Rev. 5/01)-Perf
Check only one of the below categories. L200086

- ☒ ARREST EVIDENCE
- ☐ DECEDENT'S PROPERTY
- ☐ FOUND PROPERTY
- ☒ INVESTIGATORY
- ☐ PEDDLER PROPERTY
- ☐ OTHER

DATE PREPARED: 12/17 YR 01 PCT. 079

Arresting/Assigned Officer	Rank	Shield No.	Tax Reg. No.	Command
Alberto Lozada	Det.	3497	887400	079sqd.

Date of Arrest	Arrest No.	Charge/Offense Under Investigation	Fel.	Misd.	J.D.	Viol.	Complaint No.
		Assault 3, PL 120.00	☐	☒	☐	☐	11815

Owner's Name (See Instructions)	Address (Include City, State, Zip Code, Apt.)	Telephone No.
Mitchell Rose	675 Lincoln Ave. Brooklyn,NY 11208 #18U	718-647-9086

Complainant's Name	Address (Include City, State, Zip Code, Apt.)	Telephone No.
Same as above	s/a/a	s/a/a

Item No.	Quantity	Article	Cash Value	Disposition
1	1	Brown mink coat		
xxxxxxxxxxxxxxxxxxxxxxxxxxxxxxxxxxxxxxxx				
The above is a complete list of property vouchered				Seal #2524437

TOTAL

Additional Invoice Nos. Related to This Case Including Motor Vehicles

Pink Receipt Copy of Voucher Issued ☒ Yes ☐ Refused

R.T.O. Owner/Claimant's Signature Date Time Property Clerk Storage Location

REMARKS: The above property is being vouchered as arrest evidence in connection with case#3330

Rank and Signature of Desk Officer | Tax No. 57007 | Signature Arresting/Assigned Officer | Boro Storage No.

PROPERTY ON THIS VOUCHER DELIVERED TO PROPERTY CLERK'S OFFICE BY: Rank Name Command

Property Clerk's Signature

L200086

DISTRIBUTION: WHITE - Prop. Clk. File SECOND WHITE - Invest. Unit Copy YELLOW - Prop. Clk. Work Copy
BLUE - Police Officer's Copy GREEN - Evidence Release/Invest. Copy PINK - Prisoner/Finder Receipt Copy

Mike Tyson assault report of torn mink coat

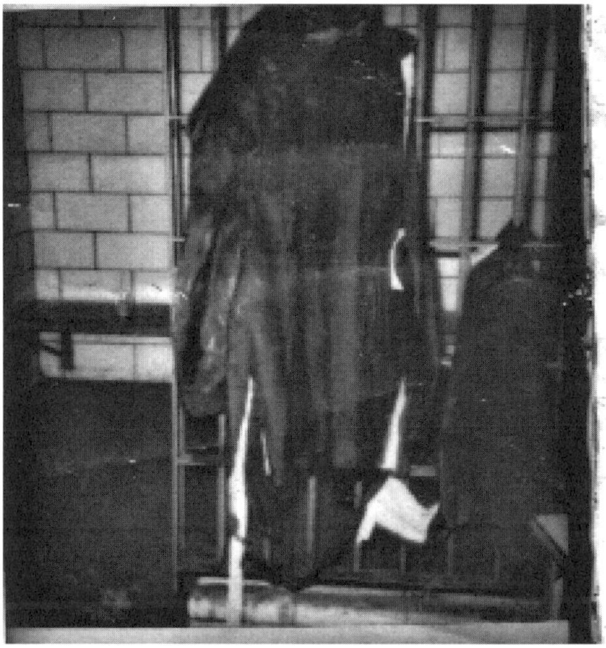

My mink coat torn by Mike Tyson

Tyson boxing's worst enemy

Has made mockery of sport

This is what I saw and why I think it happened:

The press conference to announce the fight between Mike Tyson and Lennox Lewis was a very few minutes old when Tyson looked across the stage of the Hudson Theater and mistook Lewis, the heavyweight champion, for a 19-year-old beauty pageant contestant.

The formal part of the program was about to end.

VIC ZIEGEL

Tyson walked off the platform he was standing on and began moving toward Lewis. He was inches away from Lewis' platform, the top of his head a foot below the knot on the champion's tie, when he hesitated. A man identified as Lewis' bodyguard put out his hand and brushed Tyson's chest. Tyson, mistaking the bodyguard for all the people who have kept him from living a life of quiet dignity, threw a left hand. Lewis answered with a right hand that grazed Tyson's head.

The rest, the sound and the fury, is a blur. Tyson and Lewis began rolling on the floor and, if we're willing to believe Harold Knight, Lewis' assistant trainer, Tyson bit the champion on the leg. "He's got an open wound," Knight said.

Lewis was hustled out of the theater. Maybe he needed a tetanus shot. Tyson, who stayed behind, turned to the press-conference audience and mistook it for his friends in an Indiana cell block. He grabbed that part of his body that keeps getting him into trouble and delivered a string of profanities. Look for that outtake on the DVD package of the fight.

If there is a fight.

The press release that was handed out yesterday, before the principals disappeared from view, stated the fight would take place April 6 at Las Vegas' MGM Grand Hotel. Which is where Tyson was disqualified after biting off a piece of Evander Holyfield's ear. The MGM Grand, kinder than the current economy, forgives and forgets.

But will the Nevada Athletic Commission, which was prepared to rule next week on Tyson's application for a boxing license? After the business with the ear, the commission suspended Tyson for 15 months and fined him millions. That wasn't the first entry on Tyson's rap sheet, and hardly the latest. He became another migraine for the commission after he was accused of sexual assault last September. Earlier this week, a Las Vegas police official said there was "probable cause" to substantiate that charge. Now the commission will be reviewing the tape of Tyson's performance at the Hudson Theater.

Tyson made smaller headlines earlier this month, in Havana, when he threw glass Christmas ornaments at journalists. A month earlier, a former boxer filed a complaint accusing Tyson of attacking him inside a Bedford-Stuyvesant club and ripping his mink coat. That fighter, Mitchell Rose, showed up at the press conference wearing a leopard-skin jacket and a mask over his eyes. He leaned over the balcony and screamed obscenities about Tyson until he was hustled away. He ended his stay by throwing a Ziploc bag into the orchestra, and shouting, "I wanna sell Tyson marijuana. Tell him what I told him."

We're used to that kind of nonsense. But Tyson, a former-and-potential convict, gives nonsense a bad name.

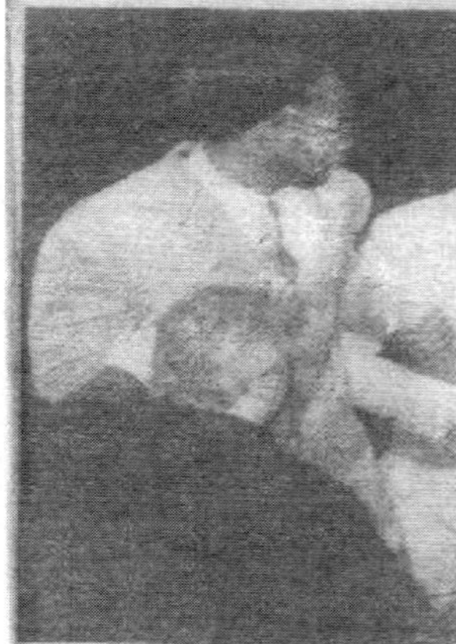

LINDA CATAFFO DAILY NEWS

Heavyweight champ Lennox Lewis is kept out of harm's way during melee involving him and Mike Tyson.

"There have been so many occasions like this in boxing and nobody's done anything," said Jose Sulaiman. "It's time to do something."

Sulaiman, who is often seen on Don King's knee, his mouth moving while the promoter drinks a glass of water, is the president of the World Boxing Council, one of those organizations that ranks fighters and collects fees to sanction title fights. He is a suspect, and a survivor, and yesterday he was part of the crowd on the floor.

Sulaiman was sitting behind the curtain when the brawl came his way. He said he was thrown to the ground, landed on his head and was momentarily knocked unconscious. "I'm very sorry," he said, "this is not good for boxing." The brawl, he probably meant.

Tyson's camp, spinning hard, said Lewis' bodyguard started it. "All Mike wanted to do was stare in his eyes, let him know, 'Here I am,'" said Stacy McKinley, Tyson's assistant trainer. "I didn't see Mike bite his foot. Lewis might have bit his own foot."

Letting them get close enough to bite and punch, if that's what happened, was a terrible idea. "I was opposed to the faceoff," said Lewis' promoter, Gary Shaw. "But Stacy and Shelly (Finkel, Tyson's manager) told me nothing would happen. They guaranteed it."

Now there are no guarantees. Only questions. Has Tyson cost himself the last great payday of his career? Will Lewis, whose only comment was a vague threat to "evaluate my options," decide to walk away?

Are you concerned, Finkel was asked, that the fight is in danger? "Of course," he said. At last, an honest man. Or am I just mistaking him for one?

E-mail:
vziegel@edit.nydailynews.com

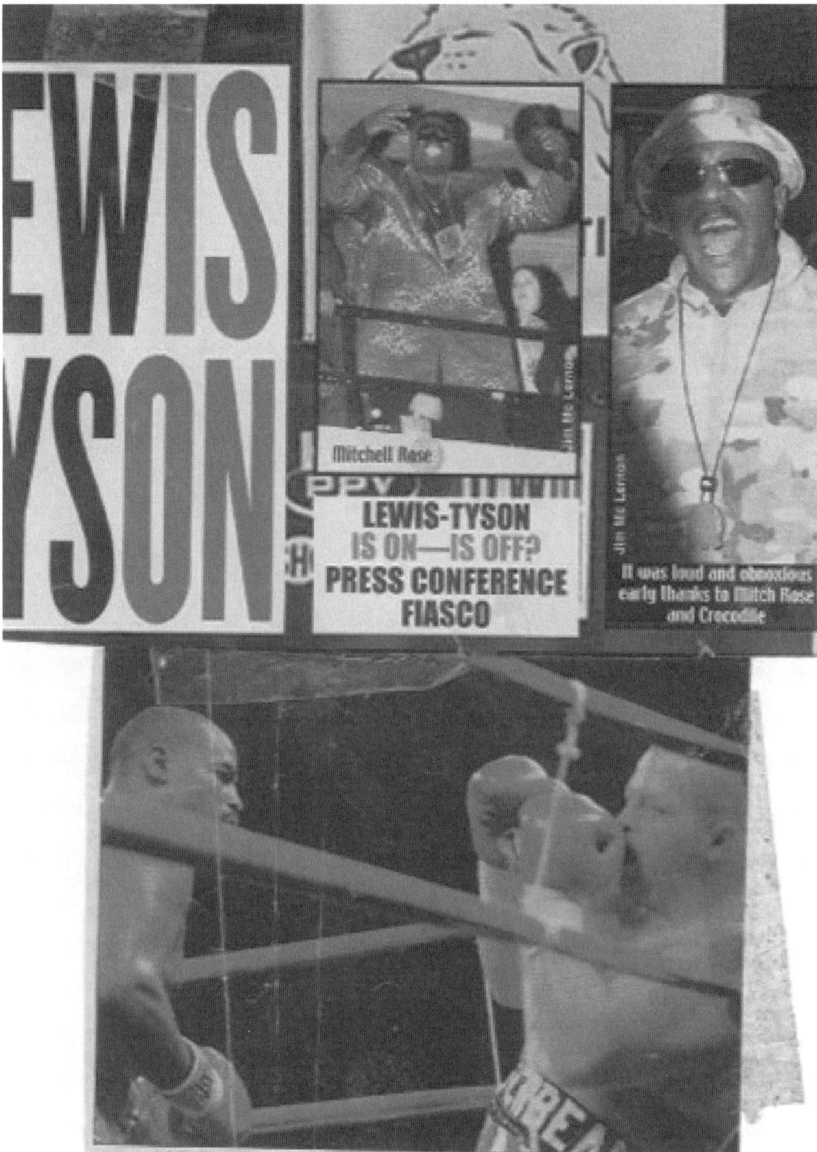

Mitchell Rose has Eric (Butterbean) Esch where he wants him

Tyson hit with slug rap

By MURRAY WEISS
and BILL HOFFMANN

An ex-Golden Gloves boxer claims Mike Tyson gave him a beating after he poked fun at the former champ's posse of women.

Mitchell Rose yesterday filed a complaint with police, charging Tyson with assault in front of the Sugar Hill Disco and Restaurant in Brooklyn. Cops were investigating, but had pressed no charges as of last night.

The melee occurred early Sunday, after Iron Mike and his entourage had sipped champagne at the club, at 609 DeKalb Ave. in Bedford-Stuyvesant.

Rose told The Post that as Tyson left, Rose quipped, "Look at Tyson. Jesus, this guy likes to talk to chickenheads!" That's an unflattering term for women.

"He heard that and it infuriated him. He came charging at me and grabbed me by the neck," said Rose, who added Tyson ripped his $5,000 mink coat and injured his neck.

Tyson's lawyer, Darrow Soll, said interviews with witnesses prove Tyson is innocent.

But Rose is firm. "It was total disrespect. He overreacted to one little lousy joke. I told Mike, 'If you want to start a holy war, so be it,' " he said.

Just 12 hours after the Brooklyn bust-up, Tyson was seen strolling Manhattan with his sister Jackie, when he gave the thrill of a lifetime to a 15-year-old boy selling M&Ms.

Stephen Smith of The Bronx couldn't believe it when Tyson approached him outside the Trump International Hotel, handed him $100 for one pack and told him to keep the change.

CHAPTER 17: SIXTY SIX MILLION DOLLAR LAWSUIT

When the district attorney finally decided to call me in for an interview, like an idiot I went by myself without an attorney. I felt I was capable of representing myself, not realizing it's almost impossible to go up against a famous celebrity without any help. With all the noise and stunts I was making, the DA had no choice but to come forward. The assistant DA who interviewed me was this nice looking lady, named Pamela. She whispered to me "Why don't you have an attorney with you?" She was gesturing, like I didn't even have a chance without one, as if she was trying to tell me something. She was drilling me with a lot of questions about the incident and was shaking her head saying to herself that Tyson was crazy but with the last question she acted offended because she considered it sexist. She asked me what is a chickenhead? I told her that a chickenhead was a broad of questionable character who is flocking around. I made up my own definition of what it meant not knowing exactly what it really meant. Her boss at the time was the main DA. He called me in his office to be interviewed. He told me I was trying to promote a fight with Tyson and that I was trying to profit off the DAs office by having Tyson arrested and that he wasn't going to let me make money off them. They didn't care about my rights being violated or about Tyson destroying my property and assaulting me, they were only worried about if I was being compensated because of Tyson's negligence and behavior. They thought that I had been drinking and deliberately gave Mike the elbow trying maliciously to start a fight.

I know they also checked out my background

with the prior arrests for the jewelry store over a decade ago and judged me by that as well. That experience taught me one thing, even when you are acquitted of a crime or violation you are still treated as a criminal. It felt like the DA was holding me by my collar and dragging me out of his office. Before I left I shouted, "Is Mike Tyson some kind of super nigga that gets special privileges or something?"

I think that in the government's eyes, there is no such thing as a second chance in life for a black man. If Tyson would have did shit like that on a white guy he would have had to pay or go to jail because the system is designed to punish you if you bother a white person. This whole situation had me pissed off. When I tried to get this first attorney named Bersnstein to come with me to the DA's office, he acted like he was afraid of Tyson's power too. The DA told me he didn't want to lose his job over this case and that it took 20 years to get his position he earned. He appeared nervous to do anything about it. In other words, he told me to take a walk. The next day I went to the bar association to attain an attorney because I felt abandoned. The line at the bar association was too long and I felt frustrated and left with my head down. When I looked up while walking down the block I saw the Supreme Court building up in front of me. I thought to myself "this is where I am going to end up if I don't get an attorney to help me retrieve my property and dignity." I then went into the criminal building loitering. While I was sitting on the bench waiting to spot a reasonable looking attorney, a paralegal was sitting beside me. I asked him what he thought about my case and if he knew of an attorney that wasn't afraid to go up against the infamous Mike Tyson. I showed him the newspaper article the Daily

News did on the story.

A lot of attorneys were afraid to be in a high profile case like this. They are afraid they could be thoroughly investigated and exposed to corruption because a lot of attorneys are into shady business practices. But this guy immediately said he knew the perfect guy for the case. He sent me to 16 Court Street to meet an attorney named Sanford Rubenstein. Mr. Rubenstein was Al Sharpton's attorney. Once the DA's office saw who was representing me, they knew I was not playing around. Rubenstein filed a $66 million lawsuit against Tyson and we both appeared in a segment that was done on Court TV.

RUSH & MOLLOY

GEORGE RUSH AND JOANNA MOLLOY EMAIL RUSHMOLLOY@EDIT.NYDAI

Legal sparring

Mike Tyson's woes mounted yesterday when he was hit with a $66 million lawsuit by former Golden Gloves boxer **Mitchell Rose.**

The complaint stems from a Dec. 16 scrape outside Bed-Stuy's Sugar Hill Supper Club that left Rose, 32, with a shredded mink coat, a sprained neck and a sore ego.

"Years ago, I always dreamed of fighting Mike Tyson in the ring, but I never expected him to attack me in the street," said Rose, a former pro boxer who sports a pair of golden gloves around his neck.

Cops have investigated but have yet to file charges in the dustup, said to have erupted after Rose called some of Tyson's female companions "chicken heads."

Abner Louima attorney **Sanford Rubenstein** is representing Rose and filed the suit yesterday in Kings County Supreme Court. Rubenstein said he has four witnesses to the fight and an MRI that shows Tyson damaged Rose's spine with a punch in the neck.

Darrow Soll, a Phoenix-based attorney for Tyson, who has been busy fending off sexual assault claims by women in Arizona, California and Nevada, dismissed Rose's suit.

"Based on our investigation, we believe the allegations are false," he told The News' **Mike Claffey**. "I think Mike [Tyson] is [illegible]"

Attorney Sandford Rubenstein and I re-enacting torn mink coat assault incident by Mike Tyson

**MITCHELL ROSE/
COURT TV INTERVIEW**

NANCY GRACE: Boxer Mitchell Rose, with his Golden Gloves around his neck, joins me right now with his attorney Sanford Rubenstein. How the heck did this happen? You always wanted to fight Mike Tyson?

MITCHELL ROSE: Yeah, definitely, you know? Mike Tyson got some type of attitude problem. I just said one comment. I just wanted to protect the guy. I wanted the guy to be aware of the young ladies he was with knowing that I had read about the sexual assaults that were pending against him. He showed me a good time so I wanted to show him I appreciated it.

NANCY GRACE: And he came at you? Now Mr. Rubenstein, you have filed a lawsuit for $66 million dollars. What are you claiming here?

SANFORD RUBENSTEIN: Well, the lawsuit has three components here. First, the injury to his body. Secondly, property damage. His coat was ferociously torn up by Mr. Tyson.
And thirdly, the most important is

punitive damages. Most of the damages are here to punish so that this does not happen again. A jury will decide how much Mr. Rose is entitled to for what happened to him. That's our system of justice and it is appropriate in this case that a jury decides for his injury, his property damages and his punitive damages.

NANCY GRACE: Mitchell, so how are you feeling now and how is your career going? Are you able to fight?

MITCHELL ROSE Well, knowing that I suffered a herniated disk in my neck, the doctor tells me that it's a possibility that if any pressure goes anywhere on that spot on the spinal cord, it's a possibility it can clog up an artery and stop the oxygen to my brain. So I'm very skeptical about fighting again. I don't know if that might be the right thing to do.

NANCY GRACE: Yeah. I'm not sure you want to take that gamble. Now, Mr. Rubenstein. Now a lot of people have gone after Mike Tyson but came away empty handed and frustrated. What makes you think you are going to win?

SANFORD RUBENSTEIN: Well, first of all, when a jury decides this case and renders a verdict, we will then collect that verdict from Mr. Tyson with the remedies allowed in the law. But first, let's let a jury hear what happened that day and make a determination in what regard to what damages Mr. Rose is entitled to.

NANCY GRACE: Mitchell, what do you think when you look at Mike Tyson? I mean, here's a guy that had it all and has had things done to him that seem to be his own darn fault. Look at him here. This is a guy who could be riding high but now he's like scraping for a place to fight. What does this do to your boxing world?

MITCHELL ROSE: Well, I just look at the guy as a guy that made a tremendous amount of money and, you know, got a lot of people around that's definitely heckling him and trying to get to his money. Maybe he made too much money for his age. I don't know.

NANCY GRACE: Some people might say you are one of them?

SANFORD RUBENSTEIN: The fact of the matter is when you go with the system of justice and allow Mr. Tyson whatever defense he chooses to raise, and to have the case decided by a jury. That's all Americans right. When they believe they have been wronged, they have a right for a jury to determine their damages.

NANCY GRACE: Yes, to stop that behavior. Mitch, don't get mad.

MITCHELL ROSE: Okay. Okay.

NANCY GRACE: We are out of time.

They called me back for a second interview. This time I had my attorney strapped to my side. The assistant DA, Pamela, jumped on Mr. Rubenstein's bandwagon and said "I am very happy to meet you." She was smiling in admiration.

The DA still played like a broker. He said that Mike Tyson admitted he did it, and he was willing to pay for my coat. The DA stated they were willing to have a press conference with Tyson and I, shaking hands, but my attorney and I had already filed my suit. The DA said that that was the best he could do, because he wasn't trying to lose his job over this nonsense.

On Court TV with Attorney Sanford Rubenstein

They let Tyson walk while I was still suffering with a numb elbow and a herniated disk in my neck which is still causing uncomfortable pain and constant aggravation. Both of these injuries required surgery which I didn't want to do. I am damn near handicapped while Tyson is hanging around buying pussy at $10,000 a pop all across the country. As for my lawyer Sanford Rubenstein, it seems as if once he used the Tyson case for publicity by appearing on Court TV, in The Daily News in Rush & Molloy's column, on CNN and other news outlets, his mission was accomplished because he knew the possibilities of winning any compensation were slim. After finding out how much debt Tyson was in with the I. R. S., Rubenstein mysteriously transferred the case over to another law firm without my knowledge. Rubenstein appeared to be the type of person that only cared about himself and money. He was so into himself that in his law office he had about 200 pictures on the wall of him posing with people and a majority of them were with Al Sharpton.

* * *

In the mist of all of this, I heard from a friend in the hood named Diaz. He told me Wendy Williams was on the radio shouting out for me to call her radio show. She wanted to talk to me about the fight with Tyson outside of the club. I called her up to tell her and the world my story. She gave me ten minutes of airtime and I did my thing. I bought a half pint of E&J Brandy and got juiced up for the show. I needed to sip a little bit to boost my courage, to be more bold in what I was saying and to talk more crazy. My mother always used to say that I talk "crazy talk." I went ballistic. I talked more shit than Muhammad Ali. I was rhyming and promoting myself for a fight with Mike Tyson.

MITCH ROSE/ WENDY WILLIAM'S INTERVIEW

WENDY: And we're calling Mitch. He's the guy.... Hi Mitch. It's Wendy Williams...

MITCH: How you doing sweetheart?

WENDY: How are you?

MITCH: Hey, I'm doing good. It can't be no better.

WENDY: Yeah. It looks like you are about to get some money. So everybody let me recap. Mitch is the gentleman who was coming out of the club in Brooklyn with Mike Tyson and apparently you and some onlookers called Mike Tyson and said why are you leaving with some chickenheads?. . .

MITCH: Well actually, I was by myself. When I go to clubs, I go by myself at three, four o'clock in the morning. I roll like that. I'm from Brooklyn so I do my rolling like that, you know? Me and Mike Tyson had a good time at the club that night. He pulled out the blunt but I didn't puff. He just puffed, him and the other crew. I don't know if that had a transreaction with the medication he was on or whatever, you know what I'm saying? But when he came out, I happened to be across the street in my 2002 Escalade parked up. You know, the diamond pearl joint parked up and Mike came out and I wanted to give him a farewell. Because I got much love and respect for Mike, I wanted to address him in the door with a farewell but when I came over there, Mike came out with these two strange chicks. I found out later they were stripper project chicks, you know, with braids and stuff in their hair, so I just told Mike, " they were stripper project chicks, you know, with braids and stuff in their hair, so I just told Mike, "Yo, be careful with those chickenheads" and Mike just got all furious and excited about it. He took it as a disrespect but as far as I'm concerned, it was something to help him. I wanted to protect him, you know, because he's the God of boxing so I wanted to make sure he's alright and to be aware knowing that I seen him that night getting a little out of control still patting and touching the butt cheeks and stuff like that.

WENDY: Right, right, right. Before we go any further, let me remind everybody that Mitch is some former kind of boxer yourself right?

MITCH: Absolutely. I knocked out that guy Butterbean, the big fat white guy that's supposed to be the Tough Man Champion. He won the Tough Man Championship a couple of times. He's about 66-1 but he refuses to give me a rematch. I have been asking for the rematch for a while. You can catch me at www. k. o. butterbeant-shirts. com

WENDY: So now did you approach Mike when the swinging started or did he come across the street and rush you at the Escalade with your mink on?

MITCH: No. I came across the street and stood on the step in front of Sugarhill and Mike was going into the white limousine and I said, "Yo Mike, be careful with those chickenheads man", you know, because I look at Mike like a regular man. I don't look at him like a God or somebody. I don't care who he is. He's just a man like me. I don't care how much money he got. I'm alright so I don't be kissing his ass and letting him talk to me any kind of way like he does with everybody else. Give me respect when respect is due and each man for himself.

WENDY: So he starting swinging on you?

MITCH: He got real excited so he ran over there to me screaming "You a disrespectful motherfucker man". The guy was screaming and pointing, so they had to restrain the guy. It took him three times to get to me. He broke out of them once then he broke out of them again. Then he ran about twenty feet then broke out of them again and ran another twenty feet so we squared off in the middle of the ring, I mean the middle of the street right in front of Sugarhill. We were face to face and Mike threw a punch, a right hand and I slipped it, and then I grabbed him, you know. Then we started tussling I kept holding because I was tipsy. I was drinking Moet all night. What can I say? So we tussling with each other and I'm saying to myself, "This guy is crazy!" I'm trying to get a grip out of him, so I squeeze out of the mink coat. As I come out of the mink coat, I back up. Then I trip and fall on to the concrete and bust my ass. I'm drunk weighing 270 pounds and out of shape not having been in the gym for a while. But recently I've been in there for three months. But I was out for a month enjoying the holiday so I was Moeted up. And Mike had all that marijuana smoke all around the place. I might have caught a contact. So you know I wasn't in a great state of mind.

WENDY: So, okay. The bottom line is you are now suing him for what a million dollars?

MITCH: Actually, I did not say anything about suing. This ain't about suing. He disrespected me in front of about fifteen people in front of the club that was laughing and heckling at me. I want to fight Mike Tyson. I can beat Mike. I'm the man from Brooklyn and Brownsville. I got the antidote to beat this guy.

WENDY: So Mitch. They say you were wearing a five thousand dollar coat. At least you want that money?. . .

MITCH: Oh, they called me for that. They told me, 'We will give you a mink coat. We'll take you and patch you up.

WENDY: Who are they? Is that Mike Tyson's camp? Because I understand they tore the coat off your back and ruined it.

MITCH: No. He didn't tear it off my back. When I came out of the coat, I tried to back up and lost my balance and fell and bust my ass and got back up. He went and picked up the coat and actually ripped up the coat with his bare hands like a caveman. He tore up the coat with his bare hands. Since he couldn't tear me up, he tore up the coat.

WENDY: So, you say all of this to say you are not suing but you are kind of pissed?

MITCH: Well, I'm pissed off. He got to pay for the coat, either or. I got it like that. He gonna have to definitely pay compensation of possibly a million or he gonna have to let me take his sister out to lunch or dinner or a heavyweight championship fight where I'm guaranteed to come out the winner, you know? That's the bottom line. We got to fight. I don't want me and Mike to kill one another or hurt one another. We can do that in the ring. But we don't want to take it to no Brooklyn thing and get all crazy and out of proportion with guns and all that bullshit.

WENDY: Alright. Well look, when Mike comes up to the radio station for an interview, I'm gonna make sure I translate that you would like to fight him plus you would like to get a million dollars and a new mink coat. I want to thank you Mitch.... .

MITCH: That's what I want. He got to give me compensation so I can go into training camp so I can do what I got to do. Because right now I'm hurting. I got a brace on and everything but I only fell. He didn't get a chance to really punch me.

WENDY: Alright Mitch. I'm gonna roll off the phone. But look,you pimp on....

MITCH: I'm gonna pimp on baby and you keep in touch and let me know what's going on and listen, check out my website. I got a song on. It's called K. O. Butterbean. It's a rap song. I want you to check it out because it's about Butterbean. He won't give me the rematch. This white guy. This Aryan that's supposed to be the superb fighter.

WENDY: Okay Mitch. You gave us the website early in our conversation so everybody got it. So I got to get off the phone, okay...

MITCH: Okay. You take it easy Wendy Williams. I love you, alright.

WENDY: Thank you Mitch. Me too.

My wife and I witt
Wendy Williams' c
Dons & Divas

Wife Delores holding down Escalade

Big Daddy Kane and I at Wendy Williams' Dons & Divas party

All the stunts that I'd pulled created a lot of tension in the neighborhood. The press conference fiasco and the jokes I cracked on the radio station and my appearance on Court TV. I even received a couple of death threats, and had a major run-in with a guy that proclaimed to be Tyson's cousin. We got into a dispute at a gas station over a pump He was really trying to start a fight with me. This was in 2002, on Flatbush, in Brooklyn, New York, in broad daylight.

When I screamed and asked him what he wanted to do, he went into his truck to get his gun. I could tell by his body language that he was going for a weapon. As he was fumbling to get his gun, I ran to my car and made it to my gun faster, and jumped over my car like Starsky or Hutch. I bent down behind my car with my gat pointing in his direction. He finally got his gun out of his stash and came out waving and screaming, "I'll kill you man! What the fuck you doin' in my territory anyway?"

I had a clear shot at him because he was wide out in the open, but I didn't want to shoot him, because people behind me could've gotten shot if he fired back. So I waved my hand as if to say, let's call a truce and put away the guns. I screamed and told him it wasn't worth it, and that we could work it out. I told him to chill and go about his business.

Eventually his friend came over, and broke up the dispute. As he was being pulled away, he was shouting, "That's why my cousin fucked you up!"

After that confrontation, I knew things were getting dangerous for me and my family so the money we were saving for our house was gonna have to be used. I went and purchased a home in Long Island. I had to get us out of the projects because I felt trapped like an easy target. People in the projects were pointing and taunting me, and saying I was about to get a lot of money because they automatically assumed that I was going to win a lawsuit against Tyson for this incident. I had thoughts about getting killed or robbed.

For the next two years, I felt like a dead man walking. I kept a gun nearby at all times, hoping that if it came down to it, I'd be able to get the first shot off. Everywhere I went, people were telling me to watch my back, but I just went on with my life. I didn't believe that Mike wanted to kill me over our disagreement. Besides we'd had a good time until that slippery comment I made. I also don't believe it was Mike Tyson that sent that guy to do that to me. It was just that people who were Mike's friends were starting beef for him. They were interfering voluntarily because they did not like the fact that I sued him and stood up to him like a man.

At the beginning, I wasn't thinking about suing or anything. It's just that after all the cover-ups, people saying I was after Tyson's money, and the D. A. treating me like a crook, I had to step up to the plate and show that I was a man too. I admit Tyson was more accomplished in boxing than I was, but I was still a man with integrity and pride. I couldn't let a rich and successful person make me feel small.

I never had any animosity toward Tyson before or even after the incident. In fact, Mike was my hero, and I love and respect him for what he did in boxing. I still believe he's one of the greatest fighters of all time. I even believe he's a better fighter than Joe Frazier and Joe Louish. The reason is because he's a modern day fighter, and he finished off the majority of his opponents in the first two rounds. He didn't have to struggle through all those rounds to make all that money. He took 300 million dollars in a flash, and that's probably why it went so fast. He's the best hustler in boxing that ever did it and he was also one of the fastest shadow boxers, even faster than the majority of lightweights.

He was always humble and never forgot where he came from. And I must admit he showed me a lot of love that night prior to the incident.

As a boxer coming up, I had always dreamed of fighting Mike Tyson. I really believed I could beat him with the right training and proper conditioning. I knew there was also a possibility that he would've killed me, so I just accepted the confrontation that we had, as my dream fight with him. I got to fight Mike Tyson and we did it "Brooklyn style." He gave me my shot, the shot I'd been waiting for all those years.

It's true that Tyson is a great boxer and an exciting fighter to watch, but how is he from a moral standpoint? I believe a true champion is true inside the ring just as well as outside of the ring. But Mike Tyson in my opinion has a serious morality issue because what he represents is unethical. Mike Tyson is a cheater that is why he bit off Holyfield's ear. He was getting his ass whipped like a dog. That is why he had his tail in his ass when Lennox Lewis was pounding on him. Mike was crying like a bitch. He is an egotistical sore loser and a spoiled brat. He can dish it out but he cannot take it. He is a soft punk motherfucker in the streets and that is why he surrounds himself with a bunch of unscrupulous gangsters and thugs. Those are his heroes so he hides behind them. And his actions are covered up and defended by top government officials and lawmen.

How dare the D.A. protect such a man as Tyson? If the police and the D.A. protect violent criminals like that it means the whole judicial system needs to be overturned. New laws and doctrines need to be established and a morality cleansing of the dictators. I thought the system was supposed to protect people from violent ex-convicts. The judicial system is so screwed up, they are giving rapists and robbers more time than murderers when life is way more precious than anything. There is not enough money in the world that can buy human life but yet you have judges out there giving brothers crazy time because they have to prove to their peers that they are not soft. And look at what they did to that kid Nick on Howard Beach that played stickball with a car thief's head. He didn't seriously hurt the guy but he was playing neighborhood surveillance and superhero. Yeah, he was railroaded!! Fifteen years! That is preposterous! I do not think that dude deserved that much time. Although there are a lot of young racist perpetrators out there, I truly believe that this was not a racial matter, this was street justice. If those guys were to be in Bed Stuy or Brownsville neighborhoods with that bullshit, and got caught by somebody in the hood they would have had a cap bust in their ass. And if he was racist, at least he did not shoot the guy. Brothers shoot other black men and only get four or five years. It's like the system is straight stacked against us because it is like nobody cares when black folks are killing each other, especially black men. I feel it is worse for a black man to kill another black man because we are brothers. A black devil is the worst devil!

I'd always been a fighter that made a lot of noise, but I never really made any money. But since I was a Golden Glove boxer and made noise throughout Brooklyn, people knew Mitch Rose. When I die a lot of people will remember me, the legend of Brooklyn, one of the best that ever did it.

Me with Sugar Ray Leonard Jr. and friends

Me with former welterweight champ Sugar Shane Mosely and former heavyweight champ Hasim Rahman at Miami South Beach

CHAPTER 18: BEST MAN WISE

Every man has his own destiny. Some of us went in positive directions and others went in negative directions but one thing is for sure, we all are going to die one day. So why don't we live in peace and harmony? I don't know why in the urban communities there is a lot of envy amongst one another. Black men are extremely jealous of one another although I believe all men are jealous of each other when it comes to the competitiveness for financial or materialistic gains. Unfortunately, brothers take things a bit too far.

My buddy "Wise" happened to be a victim of envy. Although he was a drug dealer, he wasn't a violent person and he didn't have blood on his hands. I believe he inherited some of that personality from me. He was like Robinhood: he took from the rich and gave to the poor. He tried to satisfy everybody, even his customers. He always gave back to the hood. In the neighborhood, he gave candy and dollars to the kids. He always gave a helping hand to brothers that came home from jail. He used to hit them off with like two or three hundred dollars a pop. And he did this for dozens of ex-convicts. He gave to the needy. He gave to the addicts. He used to help out the AIDS patients by counseling them and giving them financial help for medication when they needed it. They came to him because they knew nobody else would give them that support and attention and I am proud to say that he was my best man at my wedding in 1999. He appreciated my loyalty and the knowledge that I provided. He was the only friend that I knew that truly respected me and admired my style. So when he asked me to be the Godfather of his son, it was an honor to except the responsibility.

He had a brother named "World". Wise and World were both nicknames from the streets. His brother World became a very feared man in Brooklyn because of his reputation for allegedly gang banging. When people mentioned the name World, brothers started shaking in their shoes. World was part of one of the younger generations coming up in the projects that had newer views on how things were done. However, Wise loved his little brother and tried his best to keep him from getting into trouble.

I recall back in the day, this one time, World had asked me to take him to Midtown to make some money. So I took him. Wise found out about it and caught him coming off the train with me and had a fit. He began smacking World all around the train station telling him that he better not ever see him go to "Mid" again, he also screamed at me for taking him out there. After that encounter, I never took him again; although I don't know if it was for the better or worse. Eventually, he wound up in worse things than Midtown. A lot of the guys who grew up in the projects ended up committing more violent crimes like murder, gangbanging and strongarm robberies. World's whole crew started getting into all kinds of trouble. His boy, "Puerto", caught a body and his boy "Peter Rabbit" got paralyzed from the waist down then eventually died in the hospital six months later due to an infection. Then their boy "Waynno" was murdered. And a couple of his other boys got long bids in jail.

Eventually Wise got murdered by one of those same type of "new generation" young boys from the PJs. World was incarcerated at the time due to a shooting incident with the police. It is alleged that World shot at the SWAT team with an oozie. They dispersed and ran for cover and caught him later on and beat him to a bloody pulp. He was released eight months later but it broke his heart that he had been in jail when Wise was killed. It was a rumor floating around the hood that when World found out in jail about his brother's death, he started walking around the prison complaining and acting like Saddam Hussein. It was also rumored that he would not eat for days and refused to take showers. He felt it was his fault because he knew he was the one that everybody feared and disliked but knowing that he wasn't around, they took it out on his brother. World preferred to take the bullet that was really meant for him. His big brother Wise was his hero, his mentor and someone who was almost like his father.

Wise was murdered in the year 2000. He was about twenty six years old and had just had his only son. He was such a proud dad. I used to see the expression on his face when he would pick-up his son for a kiss. When he was killed, I was so disappointed about the violence in the hood that I didn't know how to react. I couldn't work or eat properly for about two weeks. I had to catch myself so that I did not lose my mind and ruin my life. I learned how to accept that he was in a better place and that nothing could bring him back. That's why by the time his funeral came, I was relaxed. I was even smiling because I knew that he was with the "Father" and in a better place with Tupac and Red Foxx.

There were a lot of theories circulating around the projects on who had something to do with Wise's death. But the alleged triggerman was a young fellow by the name of Nacho, a cousin of Peanut.

Peanut grew up with us and was also one of my digging buddies in Midtown. We all went to school together and played softball in the parks of Lafayette Gardens when we were growing up. We had good times and bad times. I remember we used to play "skelly" and "flies up" and "time out" together as kids. In Skelly, we used to shoot bottle tops filled with wax or tar to make them heavier. Whoever was the first to shoot up to 13 tops into the box won. Flies Up was a game similar to baseball except we threw the ball up against a concrete tunnel like the ones we used to crawl through when we were at the playground. And with Time Out, you had to say "time out" whenever you had candy or potato chips. If not, the snacks could be taken from you by anybody in our crew. Those were the wonder years. .

It has been speculated that Peanut brainwashed his young cousin to kill Wise. They say Nut had a grudge against Wise for an incident that was over eight years old. Peanut had a crush on Wise's girlfriend Tawana. It was said that he told her one day, "Fuck that nigger and get with this digger because if I have to, for you, I will pull my trigger." Tawana went and told Wise and Wise retaliated by pistol whipping and robbing Peanut of his jewelry. Then Wise and some other cat threw Nut down a flight of stairs in the projects. Wise told me about the incident and I told him I thought it was a little extreme but he was so in love with Tawana that he was not trying to hear anything. She was not in love with him, I knew it and I thought Peanut knew it too, and that is why he said what he said to her. Tawana used to give some indication that she was just using Wise but Wise did not care because it would be like that when a brother is making a lot of money. When I would look into Tawana's eyes, I could tell she was a snake because I watched her grow up. She was recruited by Red and Keisha the sisters of the guys Tarzan and Eyes, the same dudes that started me into criminal activity. They were gangsters and boosting bitches. Red got such a fierce reputation for stealing and fighting that Lil' Kim at one point made her a bodyguard. But I could not say much to Wise because it was not my business and he was too much in love with her to see the real Tawana. She even almost got him killed after their relationship was over when he finally realized the fraud that she was. In the same apartment he let her live with him, she sent her new boyfriend to assassinate him in. The dude came and shot up the windows on the first floor apartment that Wise resided in and tried to take him out. Wise dove for cover and ducked under the bed and narrowly escaped!

Unfortunately, the second attempt on Wise's life, the enemy succeeded. There was a lot of speculation and rumors surrounding the real reason Wise was killed. It was rumored that Peanut gave Wise a half kilo of cocaine equaling $15,000 to get shares in the L.G. Projects. But Wise and his posse tried to assassinate him in the parking lot coming out of a club to avoid giving him money for the drugs. He was scheming to keep it all for himself. It was alleged that Peanut was also jealous of Wise because at one point Peanut was large. He had won a settlement for about a half million dollars for getting shot in a club years before for an incident that he started. Eventually, the money ran out because of his flashy lifestyle. That is when he began to scheme on Wise's lucrative business in the projects of L.G. Peanut gave his cousin Nacho a package to sell in the projects but Wise told

Nacho that he was not allowed to sell in his territory. This infuriated Nacho to the point that he became vulnerable to Peanut's persuasion of murder. Being in the drug game for Wise was like a career. He refused to give up that luxurious life style, which I had introduced to him many years ago.

Wise rode around in a late model Lexus Coup which was painted money green. Brothers in the neighborhood never wanted to accept him as the kingpin of Lafayette Gardens because he was considered a choir boy from Catholic School who was a nobody not too long ago. Nacho was brainwashed that if he got rid of Wise he would be able to have shares in the projects drug trade so Nacho continued to scheme and plot. He got his excuse to kill Wise when a commotion occurred in the projects with two girls fighting in the park and Nacho was instigating the confrontation. Wise screamed on him and told him he was an aggravating motherfucker and a bum ass nigger. Then he asked Nacho as he walked by, "Do ghetto got a heaven"? With the animosity Nacho already had in his heart, it made it a fatal combination.

There was a guy in the neighborhood named Bugsy who told me Nacho had been bragging about killing Wise and World ever since he was fourteen years old. So there was animosity lingering for a long time and that is why Wise used to rank Nacho out and tease him and tell him that he was a broke motherfucker. Wise knew Nacho had some kind of animosity towards him probably because he was making money in the streets.

I even saw the destructiveness in Nacho one day. He and his cousin Peanut were in front of the project complex hanging on the corner and Nacho was throwing bottles at local cars passing by for no apparent reason. I started wondering to myself, "What's up with this guy?" He was one of those new and up and coming kids who I never really seen before, trying to make a reputation for himself. I felt from then on something was fishy about this kid. Peanut was just standing around laughing and encouraging him on his destructive behavior. This made me feel curious and leery about being around the L. G. project so I bounced. It crossed my mind that Peanut might have influenced this seventeen year old to hurt somebody but I could not put two and two together in time to warn Wise. I was not down with the drug game anymore with Wise but we remained friends throughout the years. We did not hang out with each other much but we still called each other once in a while and kept love for one another.

Coincidently, Wise called me up a week later and told me that Peanut was acting funny around him and that he thought Nut was up to something. Peanut was bringing strange dudes around the projects who were staring Wise down giving him violent and homicidal threatening facial gestures. And these were dudes with fierce reputations for hurting people in Brooklyn. I was like Wise's mentor so he called me up for advice. I did not really know what to tell him in this case other than to stay away from those projects and to not be a stationary target for anybody. I told him to be out of sight and out of mind. I did not think Peanut was thinking that violently because I watched him grow up and I never knew him to be a violent type of person. Peanut was just a pretty boy with a Macho Man Savage-type attitude, who liked to box a little and flex his muscles around the ladies. So I really did not think that Nut was going to do anything like that to Wise. I also thought Wise and Nut were cool because they sometimes talked and hung out at clubs together. I invited both of them to be a part of my wedding. On the day of my bachelor party, they were supposed to come together but instead, they drove around in Nut's Range Rover drinking a bottle of Cristal that Wise had. Wise was busy trying to keep his enemy close and make amends to Peanut but deep down inside, Peanut already had his mind made up.

When I invited Peanut to be one of my groomsmen at my wedding, he did act kind of strange. He told me he wanted to be the best man and I told him that Wise had already asked to be my best man. When I called him a week later to get fitted for his suit, he told me that if he could not be the best man, he did not want to be a part of my wedding. I was bewildered and was not sure why he was acting that way. Peanut, however, did show his support and showed up at the reception for about a half hour or so. He looked around mesmerized at how beautiful my wife looked and the scenery of the wedding. He had that look like he wanted to get married like that one day too. However, for some reason, Peanut acted suspiciously, like he was determined to complete a mission that was being planned which was the conspiracy of the eventual assassination of Wise.

Meanwhile, Wise continued his exciting life. He drove his Lexus coupe around Brooklyn all day long listening to Tupac songs. He listened to Tupac songs for six months straight and nothing else. I found that pretty weird but now I understand why he did it. It was like he knew people wanted to kill him. I wondered if he jinxed his own death. No matter what anybody would say, Wise refused to stay away from Lafayette Gardens. Even though he did not live there anymore, it was still like home to him. His business was around there so I guess he had to watch his money.

One day while playing basketball, Nacho snuck up from behind Wise and shot him in the back of the head with a 357 magnum. It was alleged that the other guys on the court with Wise - a guy named Sambo and a guy named Jimbo - scattered one way and Nacho ran down the block to a car that was waiting for him. Wise was taken by ambulance to Kings County Hospital in Brooklyn where he was pronounced brain dead three days later. At that time, Wise's mother, Ms. Harvey, decided to let them pull the plug. This was a sad day for Lafayette Gardens and the saddest part about it was that brothers in the neighborhood hated Wise and World so bad that you had people calling the hospital asking the doctors questions like, "Is that motherfucker dead yet?" It got to the point where they had to deny calls from people who were asking questions pertaining to Wise.

The actual triggerman that killed Wise, Nacho, was caught less than a month after and was eventually convicted and is now serving 16 to 20 years to life. He was convicted in the year 2000. He was only charged with manslaughter in the first degree because his defense said he was afraid of Wise and World's posse. He said he had heard rumors about them in the projects so the jury felt sympathy for him even though he blasted Wise from behind in the back of the head. That makes me wonder. Does the judicial system really think black blood is cheap?

World came home a few months after his

brother's death and it was alleged that he was walking around the city like Shaka Zulu with red blood shot eyes. And it was a coincidence that when World came home, Peanut was killed about a month later. Peanut was parlaying out in front of a club called "Club Envy" in lower Manhattan, posing with his Range Rover, most likely waiting for a shorty to come out. Some assassin crept up behind Peanut and shot him right through the back window. The bullets penetrated those pretty leather seats and hit Peanut about three or four times in the back causing him to speed off trying to take himself to the hospital. He ran over a prominent photographer and killed the man on the spot then collided into a wall and died right in Midtown where he used to do his dirt when he was a teenager.

The next day, the Daily News put in the papers that World, whose government name was Damien, the same name as the Devil in the movie "The Omen", had vowed that he would get revenge for his brother's death. It was alleged that they got that information from Peanut's cousin back in Lafayette Gardens. It was like the Daily News convicted him before even having a trial. It is kind of difficult to say what really happened that night because Nut was a trouble maker. He used to go around starting fights and all kinds of beef with people. He would do things like stare you down, step on your foot or bump you on the shoulder when he walked by like how they used to do back in 1979 to start beef. He had a knuckle game and he thought he could knock out the average Joe in the streets. Peanut thought he was some kind of muscular super hero or something.

There was a rumor in the projects that a young guy named Kojak passed Nacho the gun that he used to kill Wise. It was alleged that because of that rumor, Kojak was murdered while hanging out in the building at 456 Dekalb Avenue in Brooklyn in 2000, a week after Wise's death. There was also an old time brother from around the way by the name of Junior aka J.R., the older brother of the neighborhood bully Bush, was rumored to be the man that was responsible for being the driver in the getaway car. He was executed inside his fish and chip restaurant on Saratoga Avenue in Brooklyn. A masked man came inside the joint and pumped four shots into his body. He died in the hospital two days later.

A week later, another one of Peanut's partners was assassinated. His name was Darryl, better known as "Homicide" on the streets. It was rumored that a guy walked up on him and said, "Hey, those are some nice sneakers you got on." Homicide looked down and said thank you and then turned his head. That's when the assassin blew his head off. Then, as he was sprawled out on the ground, guys in the neighborhood who grew up with him, went into his pockets and took his money and jewelry off of him because they knew he was the type of guy who kept a wad of money and wore very expensive jewelry.

Then the word on the streets was Homicide's brother Tito came home bragging and telling people he was going to get revenge for his brother's death. Well, while Tito was working on a construction site, a man came out of a jeep and sprayed the whole construction site up with a Mac 10 mortally wounding him right on the spot and the word on the streets is that he was a very dangerous man who had a couple of bodies under his belt from the past. Five young black men were eliminated in a matter of months and the streets and media blamed it on World and his posse and eventually the FBI did the same.

They say when World came home from prison he had found some sanity. While up there he had become Muslim and found knowledge of self. Occasionally, he even started walking around with the all white Muslim outfit on and wearing the long beard and kufi. He was so feared and respected at the same time that he caught the eye of the rapper Lil' Kim at a club one day. She was on his dick so hard that she gave him her telephone number right on the spot and told him to call her. Within a month she moved him into her mansion in New Jersey and threw Junior Mafia and her crew out for him. World shocked the whole neighborhood with that maneuver and I think it aggravated the feds as well. Being with a lady like Lil' Kim made him stick out like a sore thumb even more. And it was at this time that the feds started moving in on him. Being Muslim and having a rich girl like Lil' Kim made him a threatening and feared powerful black man.

When they finally apprehended World, the Daily News said that they went all the way back to 1991 on crimes he had committed. The government charged him with crimes that were supposed to be way past the statue of limitations. Then they came to Lafayette Gardens and rounded up damn near everybody who grew up around World. They got guys who used to hang out with World, guys who just used to smoke weed with World and guys who had just come home from doing two or three year bids and said that they were down with World. They locked up this one guy named DJ, who allegedly sold drugs for World for about 2 months when he was only 15 years old. He was a juvenile. He turned his life around and was able to avoid a felony or misdemeanor. Eleven years later, the feds and Homeland Security came to DJ's house at 6am in the morning and took him straight to jail at the airport. Not a downtown facility but an airport! They eventually made him cop out to ten years in a federal prison. The feds told him if he went to trial they would bring the guy that he shot seven years ago to court and testify. This guy robbed his girl and kids at gun point and was looking to kill him back then. And two years later, all of those guys were still locked up. This is a good example on how black people are still slaves with no constitutional rights.

But before World was apprehended, he had a few missions that he completed. His first mission was to give Wendy Williams the interview she requested. One of the main reasons Wendy wanted to interview him was because he was Lil' Kim's boyfriend who had a fierce reputation in Brooklyn. Wendy gave World a lot of airtime. And word spread on the streets that World was talking about things from out of space but when I heard the interview, I thought he was dropping some serious science. But it infuriated the feds to the point that they believed that he was a nut case who needed to be taken off of the streets immediately. I called my wife Delores and told her to tune into Wendy Williams and listen to the interview. Later she said that World sounded intelligent and far from a thug, which was unlike me when I was interviewed on Wendy William's show on WBLS 107.5. When I told my story about Mike Tyson, I went bananas.

In fact, World's interview was so fascinating to the audience and to Wendy Williams that she had to re-broadcast the show after she heard he was arrested by the Feds. She had to let the people know who this guy was that made more noise than a rapper. In fact, he made so much noise, it was alleged that the interview is what prompted the feds to go after and investigate him. They always said in the hood, "Loose lips sink ships."

He "rapped" about the rap industry and about Jay-Z being a homo. He rapped about how in order to be put on in the industry you had to perform different sex acts with people of both the opposite and same sex. He also said that Nas was gay. The word around the neighborhood was that World was going around telling people that Lil' Kim was freaky. He said she liked ménage trios, gave good head and was a dyke. I guess he was angry with her after they broke up. One of the reasons they allegedly broke up is because World realized he was only being used by Lil' Kim for protection and intimidation instead of love. Lil' Kim had beef with Foxxy Brown and Noreaga and his crew. Lil' Kim sent World after Foxxy Brown's younger brother Gavin and he beat him up in a corner in the back of the club. World bitch smacked him and told him he and his sister better leave his lady alone. Lil' Kim also instigated World to step to "50 Cent" and G-Unit due to a dispute over a record Kim and 50 made together called "Magic Stick." It was a discrepancy over money that 50 didn't want to pay Kim to perform with him on stage because of the negative element she was surrounding herself with. In other words, they were leary of her man and his reputation of being a thug and a gangster.

This beef with World and G-Unit was broadcast on MTV and throughout the media. World allegedly shot at 50 Cent seventeen times. He was determined to kill him at all cost because of the confrontation with him and his girl Lil'Kim. This kind of violence brought on heat for Lil' Kim so she slowly started trying to creep away from World and his posse as the FBI started moving in but World was not letting his millionaire girl get away that easy. She already spoiled him and bought him a blue I-745 BMW and a brand new Range Rover. He also drove her drop top Mercedes Benz and Bentley all around Brooklyn. He intensified his manhandling of Kim by pimp smacking her all over her mansion (like Mike Tyson was doing to Robin Givens) while demanding money and the rights to her contract. It was alleged that World used to beat Lil' Kim so bad that she needed a facelift and a nose job. He wanted to take full control of the managerial duties. Lil' Kim couldn't handle the heat so she wanted to get out of the motherfucking kitchen! She was in too deep and that's probably why the FBI maliciously found a reason to lock her up. During the interview, World talked about fearing no man, only God. And if someone wanted to assassinate him, they'd better think twice.

After that interview, he prepared his pilgrimage to the Holy City of Mecca. He was the only black youth from the streets of Brooklyn that became Muslim in jail, and who was sincere enough to fulfill such an expedition. At least he is the only Muslim in the hood that we knew about who completed the mission.

After he completed his journey and pilgrimage, the feds were waiting at the airport terminal to apprehend him. His mission was also to join the holy war to fight against the USA. Documents in the New York Daily News revealed this fact. But he ran out of resources, so he had to come home. He hated the government and what they stood for. He felt they were part of a secret society group, and blacks were the undesirable. He also used his late brother Wise's passport to get to the Middle East. That gave him another charge on top of murder. I've got to admit,

World had the whole LG projects shook and all of Brooklyn nervous. He even had the judge nervous the one that was presiding over his pending case. The judge had to keep postponing his trial because he kept screaming and shouting at the judge saying that he was going to assassinate him.

I recall, when we were young, I got into a beef with World over an "Ice Cube" CD. That's when Ice Cube's "Amerikkka's Most Wanted" CD first came out. I let him borrow the CD and he did not want to return it so I demanded that he gave it back. He refused so I ran up eight flights of stairs to get my 45 caliber. When I came back down, I confronted a couple of his boys and told them if I don't get my CD back, I will turn the projects into a ball of fire! So World came back with his crew and surrounded the building while I was hiding behind a concrete divider with my. 45 cocked backed. However, World saw that I was serious so he decided to talk it over and return my CD. I was pleased that I stood up to these neighborhood gangsters. World and his posse are currently awaiting trial on murder, kidnapping and drug charges. The District Attorney is asking for the death penalty.

Daughter Vonnie

Daughter Delores

Me with Pastc

Bride Delores walking down isle with father

I DO!

HAPPILY EVER AFTER!

Toast to the Bride and Groom

Me with wife and mom at reception party

Wedding Party

CHAPTER 19: STOP BLACK ON BLACK VIOLENCE

It's very important for us as a people to start loving one another and caring for each other's feelings. We also need to start eating better and sticking together like the Hispanics, Jews and Italians. Black on black crime is causing a devastating effect on the urban community. Parents are losing their kids for the dumbest reasons or literally for no reason at all. And the sad part about this violence is that it has been going on in our communities since the 1800s and God only knows how long. It seems to me that when we were freed from slavery in 1865, we settled in different places but the pressure of society had turned us against each other for food, clothing and shelter. I mean, after all, most of us did not have jobs or any means of survival so I guess man's instincts were like that of an animal which was to eat each other to survive. We turned on one another for basic needs by robbing and killing.

I think this pattern of survival became evolutionary, at least, this is my theory. It is a serious bug in our communities that is floating around and it is very contagious. It's called the "flip bug." People involuntarily cross one another out of the blue because of envy or passion for another man's lady or another lady's man or for materialistic goods. It is tradition and a pattern of evolution that is uncontrollable and sometimes unavoidable. In some cases, it is taken to the extreme of death. And in some cases, it is resolved or eluded. It is one of the curses of the black man that needs to be eradicated and confronted as a disease that needs to be cured. And in my opinion, a lot of these deficiencies evolved because of slavery.

So therefore I believe reparations are necessary. If the Jews can get compensated for the Holocaust, why can't blacks get compensated for slavery? The slave trade was the backbone of America. Slaves built the railroads, the streets and highways and even contributed to the industrialization of this nation. African-Americans, most importantly, fought in the various wars for this country and are still fighting to this day with Afghanistan and still getting unjust treatment. So why won't the government admit these injustices and try to help out and make this world a better place for black people. Although there is always going to be violence, I strongly believe it could be less. We have a lot of evil people in this world and they need to be stopped quickly.

When we read the papers, all we constantly hear about is this black brother killing another black brother. Ironically, we only think about the victims. However, we never think about what the victim may have done. In a lot of cases, somebody has to be the executioner. We have a lot of criminal elements in urban neighborhoods that need to be confronted. We have friends robbing each other. We have the neighborhood murderer walking around like nothing ever happened but everybody knows about it. You got the local crackhead or common criminal who grew up with you, walked the same staircases as you and still robbed your mother while she was alone in the very same staircase. That person needs to be stopped by any means necessary because once they get away with it once, they feel invincible and they are going to do it again. And why is it that in the urban communities murders are not fully investigated as opposed to in a white person's neighborhood. It seems like when a white person gets killed, the whole world is looking for the killer but when a black person gets killed, the perpetrator is invisible and can't be found the majority of the time. When a white person gets killed, especially by a black guy, the police work more diligently using every form of technology available and the majority of the time they don't even need an eyewitness. What is this some kind of conspiracy? The government knows we should have surveillance cameras in our neighborhoods. They are whispering and not telling us or just trying to keep us in the dark and don't say or do anything about it. If you will notice, every time a murder or serious crime happens in Chelsea or Midtown neighborhoods, the perpetrators usually get apprehended. And most of the time, they show video of them committing the crime on the news. Why is that the government is protecting those neighborhoods who have less crime? While those that are statistically high in crime are left without surveillance or any kind of extra protection or deterrent security measures.

I strongly believe that we as black people have to make our communities safer by working together and not relying on the police and the government to stop violence in our neighborhoods. Nobody really makes any moves towards ending black on black crime. If "socially conscious" rappers rap about stopping the violence, they can't sell a record. If you become part of a tenant patrol, you are labeled as a snitch. If you start up an organization in the neighborhood fighting crime and drugs, you become like those Guardian Angels and nobody likes superheroes. I didn't, when I used to pickpocket in Midtown. It's ironic when black people witness a crime committed on a white person they seem to come forward and tell and cooperate, like how they told on me twice. But when a crime happens to their own kind they say "they didn't see anything" and are very uncooperative. I believe a lot of black women are spies for the white man, for example Condoleeza Rice and Anita Hill.

I have to give much love and credit to the late James Davis. He was one of the only black political leaders who tried to stop black on black crime, other than Louis Farrakhan. James happened to be a good friend of mine; we go way back. The last time I saw him before he died, he told me that he was proud of me because of the way that I stood up to Mike Tyson. I remember when he lost his job as a police officer because of his political endeavors. He used to ride around with nappy hair and dusty clothes stressed out for about a year before he was reinstated and got his police officer job back. And even when he was in that state of mind, he still organized stop the black-on-black violence rallies and movements. I used to talk to him about helping him in his crusade to stop black on black crime. He talked about a plan he believed would be effective in curbing some of the crime in our community. He called it the "reward fund."

Here's how it goes. He asked us to imagine all of those rich rappers and R&B singers and black millionaires putting money into a fund that would be used to fight murders in our community. They would put up ten thousand dollar rewards or twenty or thirty thousand or whatever amount that would stimulate cooperation from anybody that saw or witnessed a murder to come forward, not only rewards for police getting shot, but people in general. I told him that I think the rappers should be putting money into a fund like that rather than spending thousands on Cristal champagne and bling. That's the least they can do for the escalation of violence created because of all the negative language they use to sell records. I believe the black entertainers and movie stars and great athletes should be ashamed of themselves for being traders by marrying off the economics back into the white race and not acknowledging the fact that white women are only using them because they are rich and famous. There are not too many American white women who will ever really, truly, totally love a black man because the parents and relatives do not except it. That goes for Michael Jackson, Tiger Woods, Quincy Jones, Isaac Hayes, Charles Barkley, Sidney Poitier, Scottie Pippen and the rest of those folks out there. They know who they are. And O.J. takes the cake. Now white people want to put him in the motherfucking electric chair! If he would have killed two black people, he would still be commentating on NBC.

The rest of those guys should receive justice by getting the sword. Their heads should be cut off and their penis' amputated. But don't get me wrong, there is nothing wrong with fucking a white woman but marriage is an act of treason and betrayal to the black race. However, I must admit that European white women, for some reason, are a whole lot more sincere and down to earth when it comes to dating a black man compared to American white women. And ironically, the white man feels the same way about their women marrying black men. Some White men are so racist that we could be in the middle of the battlefield against Iraq, laying down shooting at the enemy and a white boy will whisper to another white boy, "I don't want to fight next to that nigger."

White men and the media try to make black men look unattractive to the white women by spreading lies and rumors that most of us have AIDS, but yet they live the same reckless life of black men when it comes to women. I know a few white boys personally I have witnessed living recklessly, especially when they have a couple of beers in them.

AIDS is affecting all races in this present day and time. It's documented that the virus is spreading in India and Russia and throughout the whole America.

Mysteriously, it started in Africa. It just seems real suspicious how all those people contracted the virus throughout a whole continent so fast. It coincidently happened in the most racist country ever, South Africa. I am not here to prosecute and convict, because the whole world is in this together now. Africa is where the real war is supposed to be. However, I must admit that blacks do have it more because of the conditions we are in, economically and mentally, because of the injustices and inequality in America, which is another form of genocide. The malicious spreading of the AIDS virus became another form of Black on Black violence that is affecting urban communities throughout the USA. Black men and Black women are knowingly spreading the virus to one another because of their victimization. They vindictively retaliate, which is causing an alarming catastrophe throughout the country. The people who commit such acts should be prosecuted to the full extent of the law. Anyone that was infected by such a person knows his intentions should turn that person in, unwillingly if necessary. This is another tacit that can help stop black-on-black violence.

As far as Mr. Davis' reward fund program is concerned, I told James that this program sounded good but it also sounded dangerous. I also told him that I had a plan which I thought would be more effective. It was called the "Surveilivision Program", which went like this. Imagine people in the projects subscribing to this program like cable. It's over 500 units in a building and if everybody paid just twenty dollars a piece for video cameras to be installed on every floor in the buildings, both elevators, in the main lobby around the parks in the project complexes, and on light poles around the whole project complex with a booth in the main building or in front of the building with a 24-hour security guard getting paid a decent salary with benefits. Especially if it's a Black or Hispanic woman, if you give her benefits she will be the most loyal third eye you will ever encounter. She will watch the video cameras religiously. This is a surveillance program that can be installed in any community and I believe it will make the criminal tell on himself. This program will also be effective in deterring the police from using unnecessary force and initiating malicious shootings when apprehending a suspect. Although it is true in some projects, that there are video cameras, most of them are placed in the wrong spots and are not fully monitored also the majority of them are broken.

With these programs, black urban communities can empower themselves and generate capital throughout America. These programs will generate more jobs and make our streets much safer. Black on black crime can be turned into lucrative business with referral fees and rewards floating around the nation giving people economic opportunities to invest in progress. Because if we going to keep losing our sisters, brothers and babies , we might as well turn it into a network of financial success which will uplift our people to a economic status as other nationalities and races.

I have been dreaming of this idea since my one year old kid almost got shot. One day my wife was walking in the building to take my daughter to see my mother and a gunman came running right beside her blasting away at this dude named Tommy. Tommy ended up shot and paralyzed from the waist down. However, during the shootout, the gun smoke and flames shot right by my wife's ear and near my baby's head. My one year old baby was actually in a real life shoot out up close. Then, when that incident happened in the park with my buddy Wise, that took the cake. The projects need serious help and attention. These incidents happened in the projects on a regular basis and the police never tried to come up with a solution. They don't even have a cop walking the beat the next day. And if they do, all the white cops are doing is looking for people's cars to write tickets and when they hear someone getting shot in the neighborhood they go the opposite direction. All the while, thinking to themselves “those niggas can kill each other for all I care, they are nothing but animals anyway”. Mean while, the black cops are busy trying to solicit someone’s wife. My wife and I were in DC one time, in an urban community and a black cop whistled at my wife right in front of me, as if to say, "So what, what are you going to do about it?" But if you are selling a whole bunch of crack vials making a lot of money, the projects will be swamped with detectives and police officers on a regular basis, 24/7, seven days a week.

I lived in the projects for almost 33 years and saw and heard it all. Everybody was around the hood when about twenty different people got assassinated in broad daylight with about twenty witnesses watching. But there is a certain protocol or code that you live by in the community that one has to go by if they do not want to be next. You got a lot of Shaka Zulu's and plenty of serial killers out there in urban communities. You also have a lot of people walking around with a lot of fear. And since blacks do not even have the right to bare arms, we cannot even defend our lives without facing severe consequences and a felony, something that will make us bums for the rest of our lives. So we are damned if we do and damned if we don't. It's like the government is sending us a message warning us that if we try to protect our lives by carrying an illegal weapon, we will receive a mandatory three years in prison. And if we don't carry a weapon, the majority of us die. Those are our two choices. Do you know how many brothers went to jail because they had a gun just to protect themselves, probably millions? And the criminals do not care about going to jail for a few years because they consider it rent free with no responsibilities so the system is doing them a favor. You have got brothers out here who cannot wait to go back to jail, a place where too many brothers act as if it is a second home. So the new gun law they came out with mandating three years in jail if a person is caught with a gun is going to be very ineffective. Only the good are going to die young. To me it seems like just another conspiracy to eradicate the black man. I do not know why they just will not draft those murderers and send them to Iraq. Because here in the United States it is like cowboys and Indians. Brothers are fighting the wrong war. The criminals have the guns and we have the spears. That means eventually brothers are going to be extinct! That is why a program like what I am proposing would save a lot of lives and prevent a lot of violence among each other. If I can save a one hundred million brothers lives and give mine, I think it will be worth it. James Davis agreed with my program but he did not think the city would allow it but instead would sabotage it.

I think people who grew up in the community knew what the community needed to stop some of the madness that was happening. Unfortunately, Councilman James Davis, was a victim of the same crime he tried so hard to stop - black on black violence. He died with a licensed gun in his possession but was still unable to defend himself. If a man can kill you in City Hall, then he can kill you anywhere. Cameras in City Hall showed how evil black on black crime is. Now we do not have a leader to keep this dream alive. A lot of people believed that his death was a conspiracy because he tried to intervene in the profitable business which is black on black violence. His assignation brought a lot of satisfaction to some White people and other non Black races. Hopefully his brother will resume and pick up where James Davis left off without letting the government discourage him by coming up with these petty prior convictions because that does not have anything to do with a man trying to make a difference in life. This mission is for God and all our fallen soldiers. This mission is also for Tupac and Biggie Smalls. Black on black crime infuriated me so bad to the point that when Jam Master Jay got killed, I went and put that same Klu Klux Klan outfit on and walked around Jay's funeral service protesting about black on black violence. The message I was trying to send was that black on black violence is not only affecting famous black people but black men all across America. And this is equivalent to us being destroyed by the Klan. Black on black crime is doing the work of the Klu Klux Klan. Remember, the Devil is always busy my brother!

Al Sharpton was my hero but he seems like he was only interested when a cop killed a black person. Then he was shouting and protesting like Muhammad Ali. Do not make this only out of a business because God has more work for you to do for the black man. And we need a lot of brothers to join together for one common cause to make things safer for our families and kids. Too many babies and innocent bystanders are getting shot. It is time to take a stand and fight back like the Muslims.

For some reason, a lot of people in urban communities think that by standing up to this type of freedom that it is some form of snitching or telling. But this isn't about snitching. This is about stopping a souped up, trigger happy punk that got away once and feels like Superman, so he will try again and next time kill. If he would have gotten confronted the first time he shot somebody, then maybe we could have saved somebody's child or father.

I am not going to be afraid to speak out about the black man living like Klu Klux Klan. The same way I spoke out about the Butterbean scandal with Top Rank and Bob Arum, I will talk about this. After all of my experiences in boxing, which eventually burned me out and discouraged me, I finally hung up my gloves like the fighters do on the TV show "The Contender." So that's why when I saw the newspaper one morning I decided to speak out. It was alleged that Top Rank, Bob Arum's company, was involved with a scandal of fixing fights. I read this story in the Daily News by Michelle McPhee so I called her up and told her that those guys did some monkey business with the belt that I won from Butterbean back in 1995. I also told her the story of how they tried to bribe me to take a dive for $5,000 to lose to Butterbean. Unfortunately, the story got blown out of context because Michelle McPhee wrote that I was cooperating with the FBI. She fabricated this story to make big headlines. The story appeared on page 2 of the Daily News. I called her back the next day after reading the article and asked her why did she tell the readers that I was cooperating with the feds. I told her "You know that's a boldface lie." I then told her that she had the whole boxing industry and people in the hood saying that I am a snitch. "What's up with that bullshit?" I asked her. She said, "Forget about those people that's talking crap. They stole your belt so do whatever you have to do to in order to get your belt back. It's your life and career they ruined. So when she put it like that, I had no comment. I just rolled with the punches. After all, it's not my fault that Top Rank employees tried to recruit a fake FBI agent and got nailed. If their organization was so legit, why would somebody in the group do something so stupid? They tried to play the game and got played. That's the bottom line. The same way they played me and my boxing career, they got played.

However, I learned by leaving the gym that it was a dreadful mistake because you pretty much abandon your body and health which is contradictory to being a true athlete. I do not think any fighter should ever totally just leave the gym unless a physical problem occurs that makes him unable to work out. After all, good health is first and everything else is secondary. After getting attacked by Mike Tyson in the street, it showed me how important it is to be in shape and conditioned at all times. I took seven years off and gained about seventy five pounds. My cholesterol started rising and health problems started coming on. It took warnings like that to make me decide to go back into the gym but it doesn't have to happen to you if you understand that physical fitness and exercise are part of life just like drinking water or eating food. So no human should neglect their body.

I am back in the gym enjoying workouts and fighting a more important fight than proving I am a champion boxer. Now, it is time to prove to myself that I am a champion in life by taking good care of my body so that I can watch my four children grow up. However, while hanging around the gym, I made a decision to take a fight in Madison Square Garden at the age of 37 years old. But I do it for fun and exercise and I do not walk around with illusions of becoming a champion in a sport that is most of the time impossible. I have hung around the game for almost twenty five years now so nothing bothers me when it comes to gym talk and voodoo worshipping on boxers. I even made a grand opening comeback with style. I sported a Mr. T. haircut. I wanted to give my fans and the boxing industry a treat. Although I lost the decision, I had fun and did not get seriously hurt. I guess for all of the things I have been through and have done, I have been sentenced to the gym for life!

I just came back to the same old foolishness that I left seven years ago, covering up my success. I fought a champion from Ireland named James Clancy who was supposed to demolish me on St. Patrick's Day. I guess it was supposed to be the St. Patrick's Day massacre of Mitch Rose because that is what they probably would have written if I let that white boy beat me up out there in the Garden. I was not having it because the Garden is special for me. That is where my career was born. I fought there about five times. When I came out to fight Clancy, I chose my entry music, a gospel song named "Victory" by Yolanda Adams. I introduced myself as "Mitch the Untouchable Rose". Clancy threw 200 punches at me but only landed ten. That is why the promoters of Irish ropes did not air my fight with Clancy on Madison Square Garden TV with all the other fights and the Main Event with John Duddy.

All the other fights were aired the next day on TV except mine. Now, you tell me what that's all about. Please tell me when you figure it out.

Rose vs Clancy fight on St. Patrick's Day at Madison Square Garden

Shop owner takes on mall developer

BY RACHEL MONAHAN

A DOWNTOWN BROOKLYN businessman is crying foul over a prominent developer's business practices.

In a lawsuit filed Monday, Mitchell Rose, owner of the lingerie business Katrina's Diary, alleges that Thor Equities engaged in "fraudulent and deceptive" activities to convince him last winter to set up shop at The Gallery at Fulton Street.

Thor representatives assured him that the mall would remain open "for many years to come," according to the suit.

Thor spokesman Lee Silberstein declined to comment on the lawsuit since they have not reviewed the case.

"Thor has not received any notice of a lawsuit," he said.

Rose is representing himself and suing for $77 million in damages, according to the suit.

Rose told Brooklyn News he was worried about signing a month-to-month agreement, but mall managers told him that the temporary nature of the leasing arrangement at the mall had nothing to do with an uncertain future.

"They assured me that it was okay – that they were just going to renovate," he said.

The mall is slated to become a massive new high rise – with a new mall, office space, apartments and possibly a hotel.

The developer, a partnership including Acadia Realty Trust, declined to comment on current evictions.

Rose, a former liquor store owner, invested almost $30,000 in setting up at Albee Square, he said, and was looking to develop his own line of urban lingerie.

Thor Equities, best known as a Coney Island developer, sold a lease for the property in June for $120 million – a heady profit, after the firm bought control of the property for $25 million just six years ago.

Rose himself said that as a former boxer he was ready for a fight and wanted to provide encouragement to fellow small business owners at the mall.

"I want to say let's fight back," he said.

Mitchell Rose

Daily News article August 21, 2007

TO ALL THE FALLEN SOLDIERS

To my grandfather Lat Henderson, my grandmother Madea Henderson, my cousin Charles, cousin Manfred, cousin Papa, cousin Shell, cousin Pooh Pooh, To all My Brothas in L.G.: aka Big Daddy Wise, aka Pretty Boy Nut, Annette aka Cruising, Shawn AKA Mays, Lil' Zeeke, Sharod, Pooh Bear, Junior H. aka JR, Lil' Wayno, Wayne aka Black, Dink, Smitty, Blue, Ron K, Ron G, - R.I.P., Hasting, Peter Rabbit, Blair from Quincy, Kojack, Homocide from N.A. Rock, Melvin R aka Frog, Norman aka Egg Bird, Bebe, Nate aka N.A. Rock, Troy aka Scareface. Hawk from East New York, Pig from East New York and Stephon aka Street Fighter, boxer Jimmy aka Rahmel from L.G. and Rab from Grand Ave.

Charles Lamar Henderson

Tribute
of
Special Days

January 22, 1974
October 19, 2005

A loving Son and brother, Defensive backs couch for Compton College, A Lakewood high school Graduate, Awarded scholarship to Virginia State University receiving a degree in sociology. #57 for the Tartans receiving All Conference Defensive End.

"CH"

THE CIGARETTE MAN

Check it out ! Check it out!
Yo! Nicotine will hit a brotha's body like some karate, Bruce Lee
Do you smoke lucies? Nigga please, that's why I eased
The mic is mine and right now I got it!
I layed off for a while and got a little rotted, but I came back from the slack
And in my pocket I got a sack of trees, I bought from my man Budsy
So a nigga kind of high 360 degrees, leaves so good they make you want to sneeze
I think I am addict because I gotta have it like the Malboro Man god damn't

CHORUS
The Cigarette Man... The Cigarette Man Those cigarettes, Man

Yo The Cigarette Man is here right now and
I am advertising them like puppy chow
Yo the Cigarette Man is here today and i got the juice
And for you I know exactly what to do
Because you dreaming and craving and feigning
Cigarette in your ear just leaning
That's why I got to get this money til it ain't funny
Be smart about it real cunning
I'm a hustler what you gonna do man take me out?
Because I make a lot of money and got a bunch of clout
Let me go over the degrees and tell you what you need
I got a couple of things I want to mail you

You can find me through the internet and send me a check
But I gonna warn you right now they can snatch it back
The federal agents will snatch up the package!
Run up in your spot and start attacking the Cigarette Man

CHORUS
The Cigarette Man....... The Cigarette Man
Those cigarettes Man

Yo the Cigarette Man is here to stay and
I'm confident he ain't going away
So those lucies you be coping gonna be around
They can't stop them
Like they did in Riker's Island in jail second hand smoke you inhaled
They got them everywhere America don't care
So homeboy I suggest you be aware
Cause you making your health hazard
So I gonna tell you man you need to quit
The Cigarette Man is not not going
Even if its raining or snowing
Nigga's don't care outside if its cold
And I'ma tell you right now my name is Mitchell Rose
I'm the Golden Glove contender
I was a winner!
But they stole my gold so I'm back on the road
Yo! that midnight train to Georgia
And I'ma tell you right now, girlfriend, I can afford ya
I take paper, I take plenty dough!
I take it fast never slow
I be taking like a gardener be raking
So if you scared go get a dog because I don't be

faking
I been doin' this since I was seven
Righteous god body going to heaven
I'm Big Un I like to have fun and I came to the party til the job is done
Because right now it's undone and I have to do it
So me and my man Budsy is here to step to it
The business seriously taken
Because somebody has to bring on the bread and bacon
Newports, Cools, Cools Light, Benson Hedges is what my mama used to like
Malboros they alright, make a White boy scream DYNOMITE!
Winston Salems you inhale them
And throat cancer is one of the leading causes of death
So I suggest you quit if you want to maintain good health

CHORUS
The Cigarette Man.....The Cigarette Man .....Those cigarettes Man ...

ORDER FORM

ROSE KNOCKOUT PRODUCTS, INC.
P.O. BOX 691
VALLEY STREAM, NY 11582
MitchRoseBoxer @hotmail.com
myspace/Mitchell Rose
Videos on Youtube.com/Mitchell Rose

NAME:____

ADDRESS:_____________________________________

____

CITY/STATE ZIPCODE:

____

____

Form of payment:
Institutional Checks, Money Orders, Credit Cards